José Ignacio Rodríguez, Thomas Jefferson Durant

**United States and Spanish Commission**

José Ignacio Rodríguez, Thomas Jefferson Durant

**United States and Spanish Commission**

ISBN/EAN: 9783337379308

Printed in Europe, USA, Canada, Australia, Japan

Cover: Foto ©Suzi / pixelio.de

More available books at **www.hansebooks.com**

# UNITED STATES AND SPANISH COMMISSION.

## A REPLY TO THE PAMPHLET ENTITLED "VIEWS OF THE ADVOCATE OF SPAIN AS TO THE RIGHTFULNESS OF THE EMBARGO OF THE PROPERTY OF AMERICAN CITIZENS IN CUBA."

Under the title of "Remarks on the embargo of the property of American citizens in Cuba," the advocate of Spain has published in pamphlet form an argument addressed to the arbitrators and umpire of this commission, with the design of showing that the embargo of the property of American citizens by the Spanish authorities in Cuba was not in conflict with the treaty between Spain and the United States of 1795 (see argument of advocate of Spain, p. 56, foot, and 59, top), and that such embargo, moreover, was justified by the examples alleged by him to have been set by the legislation of the United States during the war of the rebellion.

The learned advocate of Spain had, in a previous pamphlet, contended, as he does in this, that no native of Spain ceases to owe allegiance to that government by reason of his naturalization in the United States. (See present argument of advocate of Spain, p. 2.)

The reasons which have addressed themselves to the mind of the advocate of Spain, and led him to these conclusions, certainly never presented themselves to the minds of the representatives of Spain and the United States who framed the convention of 1871, for had they been presented the convention never would have been made, since, under such views, there would then have been little or no need of it.

It is unnecessary to repeat here what has already been said by the undersigned in the reply made by him to the pamphlet of the advocate of Spain on naturalization, and which reply is in the hands of the members of the commission. Reason and authority must have lost their force if the law and decisions there quoted do not demonstrate that a naturalized citizen of the United States owes allegiance to this country, and to this alone.

With regard to the embargoes in Cuba of property, real or personal, of citizens of the United States, we must first look to the terms of the convention of 12th February, 1871, and find what light is thrown upon the subject by its language and the contemporaneous exposition which it may have received. These will be found to stand in the most direct opposition to the views announced by the advocate of Spain.

The agreement between the United States and Spain of February 12, 1871, for the settlement of certain claims of citizens of the United States speaks in its opening phrase of claims of citizens of the United States, or of their heirs, against the Government of Spain for wrongs and injuries against their persons and property, and declares that all such claims shall be submitted to arbitrators. These expressions are general and comprehensive, embracing every conceivable injury

1 SP

that may be done to a citizen of the United States, or to his property, by any authority of Spain in the island of Cuba, and there are no expressions to be found in the entire course of the agreement placing any limit upon these wide and ample terms. Every species of wrong or injury to property is included; whether it be inflicted by waste or destruction, by seizure and detention, by sequestration or confiscation, by embargo or otherwise, such wrong and injury, by the terms of the agreement, are a subject for the jurisdiction of the commission.

The agreement of 1871 is complete and self-sufficient by its own terms; the wrongs and injuries demanding redress are clearly pointed out, and a tribunal constituted to hear, adjudge, and afford remedy and satisfaction. It is manifest, therefore, if it could be demonstrated, as it cannot, that other agreements and treaties previously existing between the high contracting parties did not provide remedies for certain special wrongs and injuries to persons or property, such a demonstration would be immaterial, since this convention of 1871 provides for all wrongs and injuries, and so fills up any omission which may exist in any other and previous treaty. And therefore it is scarcely necessary to inquire whether the philological discussion entered into by the advocate of Spain in regard to the meaning of the word "embargo," as used in the English and Spanish texts, respectively, of the treaty of 1795, be well applied or not, for whether he be right or wrong the fact remains that the wrong done to property by whatever name you may call the act of seizure, whether embargo or sequestration, is covered by the agreement we are acting under.

It may not, however, be immaterial to observe that the original treaty of 1795, as it now exists in the United States Department of State, is signed on the Spanish portion of the treaty, as well as the English, by "the Principae de la Paz," Manuel de Godoy, and this fact proves conclusively that the word "embargo" was used in the treaty in its full Spanish signification, and with all the varieties of meaning which it enjoys in the Spanish language, which, had there been any design to limit, the intention would have been expressed at that time, and in the absence of such expression no restriction can be maintained to exist.

Domingo Dulce, as the appendix to the argument of the advocate of Spain shows, on the 17th of April, 1869, had placed an "embargo" on the property of sixteen individuals, simply by his own will and by that alone. He appointed a board to administer this property. He excluded the judicial tribunals from the power of construing and interpreting questions that might arise under the administration of this board. By his order three days subsequent he applied this "embargo" system to all persons who, as he or his subordinates might see fit to suppose or declare, had taken part in the insurrection directly or indirectly, in or out of the island, either armed or aiding the same with arms, ammunition, money, or provisions; all of whom were deprived of all *civil and political rights*, or in other words were, without form of trial or of law, pronounced and liable to be treated as outlaws.

Under these despotic orders, a number of citizens of the United States residing within our limits, but owning property in Cuba, were at one blow stripped of such property, and by the sentence of a court-martial condemned to death.

These are matters which the advocate of Spain contends the United States has no right to complain of, and grounds his contention on the assertions that such measures were, in the judgment of the Spanish authorities, necessary, which is mere arrogance; and that they were justified by the examples set by the United States, which is simply untrue.

The history of events which followed these extraordinary decrees, embargoes, sequestrations, and confiscations in Cuba is well known. Our government remonstrated at once, and after some negotiations the agreement constituting this commission was adopted.

These negotiations show the contemporaneous understanding of the two governments as to the conduct and the language of the Spanish authorities in Cuba.

On the 24th June, 1870, Mr. Fish, Secretary of State of the United States, instructed Mr. Sickles, minister of the United States at Madrid, to bring to the notice of the Spanish Government the claims of citizens of the United States against Spain growing out of summary arrests and imprisonments, military executions, *arbitrary embargoes of property*, and other acts done by the Spanish anthorities in Cuba to the persons and property of citizens of the United States in violation of the treaty of 1795. (See papers relating to the foreign relations of the United States, transmitted to Congress with the annual message of the President, December 4, 1871, page, 699.)

Here it is seen Mr. Fish treats the "embargo," of property under Dulce's order in Cuba, as the same thing as the "embargo" mentioned in the treaty of 1795.

In his note to Mr. Sagasta, Spanish minister of state, July 26, 1870, Mr. Sickles expressly refers to and quotes the 7th article of the treaty of 1795, forbidding "embargoes," as being violated by the orders of Dulce. (Same volume, page 701.)

In the answer of Mr. Sagasta, the same argument now employed by the advocate of Spain was put forward, in an attempt to show that the Article VII of the treaty of 1795 did not apply to Dulce's embargo (same volume, p. 711); but this argument was conclusively met by Mr. Sickles's reply, in the course of which he employed the following language: "Although, as I have already remarked, the admission of your excellency that it is unnecessary to rely upon the special stipulations of a treaty to exempt a foreigner from the operation of the decree of embargo renders it superfluous to proceed with the discussion of the seventh article of the treaty of 1795, in its relation to that proceeding, I must not refrain from expressing my dissent from the construction given by your excellency to that article. The first clause is the one which relates directly to the questions now under consideration. It is as follows: 'And it is agreed that the citizens or subjects of each of the contracting parties, their vessels, or effects, shall not be liable to any embargo or detention on the part of the other for any military expedition or other public or private purpose whatever.' Your excellency contends that the estates embargoed have not been taken for any of the objects expressed in the clause cited, and that therefore it has not been violated. If it is meant that the property embargoed has not been taken or detained for 'any military expedition,' and that consequently this provision of the treaty has not been contravened, I must remind your excellency that the prohibition extends to every possible 'public or private purpose' to which an embargo may be applied. The embargo enforced in Cuba is described by your excellency as 'an extraordinary means of defense,' adopted by the authorities 'to deprive the insurrection of powerful resources.' It is, then, a military measure, intended to strengthen one party to a conflict and weaken the other. It would therefore seem to be fairly embraced in the particular prohibition relating to military operations, as it is certainly comprehended in the general interdiction of embargoes for any 'other public or private purpose whatever.' Your excellency is pleased sometimes to regard the embargo

4

in Cuba as a punishment for a crime—that is to say, a judicial act; at others your excellency describes the proceedings as only a preventive measure of a purely political character; and, again, it is called an extraordinary means of defense, having for its object to deprive the insurrection of resources. But a further and more practical demonstration of the character of the embargo in Cuba is found in the decree of His Highness the Regent, dated on the 12th instant, and published in the Gaceta of yesterday. It is therein provided that the proceeds of the sales of embargoed property in Cuba are to be applied toward the support of the government of the colony for the current year. Examined in any aspect, whether military, political, or legal, no justification has been found for the manner in which the executive authorities in Cuba have sequestered the property of American citizens. If the object is to punish offenders against the laws, be it so; then the accused are entitled to a judicial hearing before judgment is pronounced against them. Yet it is confessed that the courts of justice have not been consulted, and that no law authorizes these acts of confiscation. And if by a measure of defense or prevention, whether political or military, it is meant that, in order to diminish the means of the insurgents and to augment the resources of the Spanish treasury, the property of citizens of a friendly nation, not residing within Spanish jurisdiction, may be seized and sequestered, I must insist that the mere statement of the case discloses a palpable violation of the immunity belonging to the property of aliens, from which a right of release and indemnity follows as a matter of course." (Same vol., p. 725, foot.) After this the view presented by Mr. Sickles does not appear to have been controverted at Madrid (see Mr. Sagasta's letter to Mr. Sickles, same volume, pp. 744, 745), but was directly acquiesced in by Mr. Martos, the successor of Sagasta.

Thus it appears that by the understanding of both governments the embargo or sequestration of the property of American citizens in Cuba was considered to be an infraction of the treaty of 1795; but even had that consideration not entered into the subject, the agreement of 1871 would suffice, since, by the terms then agreed upon, Spain undertook to pay pecuniary damages to those citizens of the United States who had thus been injured in their property.

So the cases brought before the commission have complained of the embargo as an injury in itself, and as a violation of the treaty of 1795, and they have been treated and decided from the beginning in that sense. The contemporaneous exposition of the agreement, and the precedents established under it, show conclusively that the view presented by the advocate of Spain is erroneous. The following cases have been decided in the commission, and recognize the liability of the Spanish Government for the full amount of damages suffered in consequence of the embargo of property of claimants as an infraction of the treaty of 1795, and as provided for under the agreement of 1871:

No. 13. J. G. De Angarica.—Decided by umpire November 2, 1875, with an award of $748,180.

No. 14. Gideon Lows.—Decided by umpire December 12, 1874, with an award of $175.

No. 31. J. M. Delgado.—Decided by umpire February 27, 1875, with an award of $113,360.

No. 32. Fernando Dominguez.—Decided by arbitrators October 4, 1879, with an award of $1,500.

No. 41. José de Jesus Hernandez y Macias.—Decided by arbitrators January 26, 1875, with an award of $3,000.

No. 66. Gonzalo Poey.—Decided by arbitrators April 8, 1876, with an award of $313.75.

No. 96. Youngs, Smith & Co.—Decided by umpire November 20, 1879, with an award of $13,600.

Thus, again, we have the meaning of the agreement settled by this course of decision, which the plainest principle of reason and justice demand should remain undisturbed.

It is further contended by the advocate of Spain that a state of war existed in Cuba similar to that which existed in the United States from 1861 to 1865; that such state of war in Cuba justified the seizure of the property of American citizens residing in the United States, who were believed by the Spanish authorities to be giving aid and comfort to the insurgents; that such seizures were justifiable, because, adopted for the purpose of suppressing the insurrection, were not contrary to international law; and were further justified by the example of the United States during the war of the rebellion; from all of which the advocate of Spain infers that the only indemnity citizens of the United States are entitled to is the restoration of their property without damages, or its net proceeds in cases where it has been sold.

The premises from which these conclusions are drawn by the advocate of Spain are not supported by the facts of history.

The Spanish authorities never admitted and always denied the existence of a state of war in Cuba; nor was it ever recognized by the United States or by any European nation. This is shown everywhere in the official correspondence between the United States Government and that of Spain. Admiral Polo de Bernabé, the Spanish minister here, in his letter of 30th December, 1873, to Mr. Fish, in relation to the case of the Virginius, said, "With respect to all these matters, the undersigned cannot but confidently expect the admission on the part of the Secretary of State, that the obligations of one power toward another friendly power, in whose territory there exists an insurrection *to which neither party has granted belligerent rights* in an international sense." (See papers relating to the foreign relations of the United States, transmitted to Congress with the annual message of the President, December 6, 1875, vol. ii, page 1155.) And in his answer to this letter Mr. Fish said (see same vol., p. 1158), " Spain, in advancing the present reclamation, does not admit that there is a state of war, and does not pretend to represent injuries of subjects of hers preyed upon by the Virginius as a cruiser."

But in the United States, in the war of the rebellion, belligerent rights were recognized from the beginning, as pertaining to the insurgent States of the South. As soon as the news of the attack on Fort Sumter was known in Europe, the Government of Great Britain issued, on the 13th of April, 1861, a proclamation of neutrality, "recognizing hostilities as existing between the Government of the United States of America and *certain States* styling themselves the Confederate States of America." This was followed by similar declarations from other European powers. Hence there were two belligerents, for that is the meaning of a proclamation of neutrality.

The United States Government proclaimed and acknowledged the state of war by its blockade of the coasts of the Confederate States, by exchange of prisoners, by negotiations, and in other ways.

The advocate of Spain, in order to support, against the constant declarations of his own government, that a state of war existed in Cuba, asserts that "about the 1st of October, 1868, a portion of the population of Cuba rose in arms and made war upon the government of the island, with the avowed purpose of throwing off the dominion of Spain";

and states further, that "the insurrection speedily obtained great proportions." How correct this may be is shown by the statement of Admiral Polo de Barnabé, in his letter to Mr. Fish, February 2, 1874, same volume quoted above, p. 1165, when he said, "The insurrectionary rising which took place at Yara, in 1868, did not find extensive sympathies in the island of Cuba, and, although the superior political authority was badly provided as regarded the question of material force for encountering that traitorous manifestation, it was but a little while before its locality was limited to the eastern part of the island," where, as the consul, Mr. Hall, wrote to the Secretary of State, Mr. Seward, on the 18th November, 1868, "the wild nature of the country, and the complete absence of railroads and even of ordinary roads, militated greatly in favor of the insurgents." And on the same page the admiral says, "The want of popular support, before alluded to, and other causes, reduced the insurgents in the eastern extremity of the island to the condition of wandering bands, destitute of arms and munitions of war, with no other access to the ports and places where it was possible to communicate with countries beyond the gulf than those which temporarily, and under certain circumstances, may be held by parties of bandits or rebels in all parts of the world."

This is the situation which the advocate of Spain, contradicting his own government, depicts as a state of war in a national sense, and compares with the civil strife in the United States, where the insurgent government included eleven organized States, with an area of upwards of 745,000 square miles, and a population of 12,000,000, sending nearly one-twelfth of that number into the field, and commanding the sympathies of the European governments, manifested in their proclamations of neutrality and otherwise. The comparison seems to border upon the absurd, though gravely insisted upon by the Spanish advocate.

Nor does the manner in which the insurrection was treated in the two countries stand in a less striking contrast. The Spanish authorities in Cuba, although there was no war, and as consequently there was peace, proceeded at once in time of peace to exercise war powers unknown to civilized nations.

On the 24th March, 1869, the captain-general of Cuba issued a decree which declared, among other things, that "vessels which may be captured in Spanish waters, or on the high seas near to the island, having on board men, arms, and ammunitions, or effects that can in any manner contribute, promote, or foment the insurrection in this province, whatsoever their derivation and destination, after examination of their papers and register, shall be *de facto* considered as enemies of the integrity of our territory, *and treated as pirates*, in accordance with the ordinances of the navy. All persons captured in such vessels, without regard to their number, will be immediately executed." (!) This decree moreover was carried into execution.

On the 4th of April succeeding the promulgation of this decree, another was issued by Count Valmaseda, which declared—

1. "Every man, from the age of fifteen years upwards, found away from his habitation (finca), and does not prove a justified motive therefor, will be shot."

2. "Every habitation unoccupied will be burned by the troops."

3. "Every habitation from which does not float a white flag, as a signal that its occupants desire peace, will be reduced to ashes."

These decrees amazed the civilized world. They were no idle threats. Hundreds were put to death under them.

It is to such decrees, ordering the burning of uninhabited houses, that the advocate of Spain compares the legislation of the United States, which directs abandoned property to be properly cared for, and such as was of a movable character to be sold and deposited in the Treasury to await the claim of loyal owners, as was directed by the provisions of the act of 12th March, 1863, with regard to abandoned property in the insurgent States.

Here it is important to direct attention to the remarks of the advocate of Spain in regard to this legislation of the United States during the war of the rebellion, for the purpose of correcting the erroneous impressions which the views he presents are calculated to impart.

The legislation referred to consists of the following :

The act of August 6, 1861, 12th Statutes at Large, p. 319, "An act to confiscate property used for insurrectionary purposes."

The act of July 17, 1862, same vol., pp. 589 *et seq.*, " To suppress insurrection, to punish treason and rebellion," &c.

The act of March 12, 1863, same vol., p. 820, " To provide for the collection of abandoned property," &c.

These are laws passed by the Congress, and were not mere acts of the executive, such as the order of the captain-general in Cuba, issued in defiance of law.

The acts of August 6, 1861, and June 17, 1862, provide for regular proceeding in the ordinary judicial tribunals of the United States, not in military courts.

The act of 12th March, 1863, provides that abandoned property of a movable character shall be gathered and sold, the proceeds put in the public treasury, and the government to hold them in trust for the loyal owner.

This latter act especially the advocate of Spain places in a distorted light, by quoting the case of Molina, reported in the sixth volume of the Court of Claims. He says, " How many Spanish subjects had their property taken and disposed of under those acts it is needless to inquire. It is enough that in the case of Molina, reported in volume 6 of the Court of Claims, that court decided that Spanish subjects were within the provisions of the act of 1863, and so entitled only to the actual net proceeds of their property without interest."

Now to compare this case of Molina with the embargo in Cuba of the property of American citizens is a total misapplication of facts.

The property of Molina, when taken, was not known to belong to a Spanish subject, nor was it known to be such when sold and the proceeds placed in the national treasury. It was property abandoned by the owner, whose name and quality were unknown ; and it was not taken because the owner was a Spaniard, as property in Cuba was taken because the owner was American. When Molina found that his property had been thus taken and sold, he had to consider, and of course did consider, whether or not it had been taken in violation of the seventh article of the treaty of 1795. He concluded either that it was or was not taken in violation of that treaty. If he concluded it was not taken in violation of that treaty he had nothing to complain of. The United States had taken his property when abandoned and liable to destruction, for the rebel authorities burnt all cotton they could not export. His cotton had been converted into money; his twenty-four bales procured him, by the judgment of the court, the elevated price of more than one hundred dollars a bale. But suppose that he had come to the conclusion that his property had been taken in (unconscious) violation of the treaty rights of a Spanish subject. In that case he could have appealed to his government for redress. He chose not to do so, but to appeal to ours. Where is the injury ? He claimed no rights under the treaty of 1795. A reference to the case, as reported, will show that but two questions were contested, and both were decided in Molina's favor. These questions were whether the fact that he had joined with him a coplaintiff who had no interest in the cotton made any difference; and whether an American citizen could sue the Spanish Government in the courts of Spain, which was the condition upon which Spanish subjects could sue the United States in the Court of Claims. As we have said, both questions were decided in Molina's favor, and the court expressly said in the conclusion of its opinion (page 278) that there was "no other question of contest in the record."

It would be difficult to find a case more unlike than this of Molina to the seizure of the property of American citizens in Cuba, when examined before this international commission.

The labors of the undersigned have been greatly lightened by the aid of the author of the subjoined letter, Mr. J. I. Rodriguez, formerly a judicial functionary in the island of Cuba, now a highly respected member of the bar of New York and of the Supreme Court of the United States. To this letter, giving a complete and lucid view of the question of embargo and of the situation of affairs in Cuba during the recent contest, the attention of the arbitrators and umpire is respectfully invited.

February 18, 1881.

THOMAS J. DURANT,
*Advocate for United States.*

REMARKS OF J. I. RODRIGUEZ ON THE PAMPHLET PRINTED BY THE ADVOCATE FOR SPAIN, EXPRESSING HIS VIEWS AS TO THE RIGHTFULNESS OF THE EMBARGO OF THE PROPERTY OF AMERICAN CITIZENS IN CUBA.

To the Hon. THOMAS J. DURANT, *Advocate for the United States in the United States and Spanish Commission:*

The "*Views of the advocate for Spain as to the rightfulness of the embargo of the property of American citizens in Cuba,*" which are the subject of the pamphlet of 80 pages with which he has enriched the juridical literature of this country, are met *in limine* with a fatal objection.

It is in vain that the advocate for Spain has undertaken to write history, and describe in his own way the "*outbreak of the insurrection*" of Cuba, the "*devastation of the island by the insurgents,*" the organization of "*the junta in New York,*" and the "*position of the native Cubans,*" both here and in Cuba.

I might tell him in answer to these four chapters of his pamphlet:

(*a.*) That the outbreak of the insurrection in the island of Cuba has had the unusual good fortune to find justification and even applause on the part of those who had themselves the greatest interest in suppressing it; such as Marshal Serrano, General Dulce, President Castelar, General Prim, and a host of Spanish statesmen (see note No. 1); and that therefore it was not the result of "*a semi-insane spirit of chronic rebellion,*" as he has stated.

(*b.*) That the devastation of the island by the insurgents was purely a measure of war, like the devastation of the South by the "great march of General Sherman," and like many other devastations which unfortunately had happened in the world; and, further, that it was resorted to only as reprisals for the celebrated infamous proclamation of

9

the 4th of April, 1869, issued by the Count of Valmaseda, then the general-in-chief of the Spanish troops, against which the President of the United States directed his Secretary of State to protest in the name of "*Christian civilization and common humanity.*" (See note No. 2.)

(c.) That the "Junta in New York," which he is bold enough to say enjoyed "*the hearty sympathy of the President of the United States and all his Cabinet,*" and would have continued to enjoy it "*had it employed its money and energy in a manner equally inimical to Spain, and probably more dangerous to the peace of Cuba,*" if something had not been done by it "*contrary to the laws of the United States,*" was for this same very reason an organization which by itself did not violate the laws (unless the purpose of the advocate of Spain is to impeach General Grant and all his Cabinet, and accuse them of being in hearty sympathy with illegal organizations); and which, as soon as the President deemed it proper to declare by proclamation, according to the humane and civilized manner of doing things in this country that the said organization should cease to exist, disbanded itself immediately, and promptly obeyed the orders of the head of the nation. (See note No. 3.)

(d.) And, lastly, that the position of the native Cubans, whom the advocate of Spain has never had the honor to know, far from being that of "*deadly hatred,*" which he supposes without more foundation than the paid utterances of mercenary parties, was always before the insurrection that of the best and most faithful Spanish subjects (see note No. 4), and after the insurrection that of men who are fighting to conquer their independence, and determined to die with honor before losing their dignity (see note No. 5); and furthermore, that if such a *deadly hatred* had existed, the Cubans who could have still laid waste the whole island, and ruined Spain forever by burning the comparatively few plantations which remained untouched, and by creating agitation among the slaves would have not accepted the capitulation proposed to them by the great modern captain, Marshal Martinez Campos, and would not have devoted themselves, as they are now doing, to reconstruct the country, abolish slavery in a peaceful way, and enjoy those Spanish liberties of which they had been wrongfully deprived.

All of this I might say to the advocate of Spain, not upon false information or incomplete study of historical events, but upon full, correct knowledge and authentic documents ; but all of this would be useless to a certain extent, because even if the advocate for Spain were correct in his *views* about the "*outbreak of the insurrection,*" the "*devastation of the island by the insurgents,*" "the junta in New York," and the "*position of the native Cubans,*" nothing of this kind would be of any value at all to demonstrate that the "embargo of the property of American citizens in Cuba" was *rightful.*

It may be that the idea of the advocate is that Spain had the right to punish in this way *American citizens* having property in Cuba, because of the "*hearty sympathy of the President of the United States and all his cabinet,*" towards the insurrection. I might find myself supported in this idea by the perusal of his fifth chapter (page 12), on the "*negotiations of the United States in regard to Cuba.*" But I should say in this case (after admiring again the patriotism of the American lawyer who endeavors to criminate his own country before the eyes of Spain), that the right thing for Spain to have done was, not to seize the property of other American citizens, but to seize the property of General Grant, of Mr. Hamilton Fish, and of all the other members of the cabinet, or try them by a council of war, and condemn them by default to death and confiscation of property.

However guilty might have been President Grant and all his cabinet of hearty sympathy for the Cuban junta, this is not a country in which the people may be held responsible for the acts of the heads of the government, because the people here is the sovereign, and the heads of the government the servants of the people; nor was it right for Spain to punish innocent persons instead of punishing sinners In the Spanish language there is a maxim to this very purpose: *No deben pagar justos por pecadores.*

But I have said that the whole pamphlet of the advocate of Spain falls to the ground in the very threshold of the discussion, because independent of the treaties, and independent of all other considerations, there is a Spanish law, which the advocate for Spain has not read, or if he has read it, has not cared to remember, forbidding *in toto* these *embargoes*, the rightfulness of which he is attempting to prove.

This is the law of September 28, 1820, enacted in Madrid, communicated to Cuba, and inserted as " transmarine legislation," in the well known Zamora's BIBLIOTECA, vol. III, page 218, word EXTRANGERO.

The fourth article of this law reads as follows, in Spanish.

ART. 4°. *Ni á título de represalias en tiempo de guerra, ni por otro ningun motivo, podrán confiscarse, secuestrarse, ni embargarse dichas propiedades* (las propiedades de los extrangeros en España); *á no ser las que pertenezcan á los gobiernos que se hallen en guerra con la nacion española, ó á ñ sus auxiliares.*"

Or in English:

"ART. 4th. Not even by way of reprisals in time of war, nor for any other reason whatever, shall it be lawful to confiscate, sequestrate, or embargo the said property (the property of foreigners in Spain); but it shall be lawful to do so when the property belongs either to the governments with which the Spanish nation is at war, or to their allies or auxiliaries."

We see therefore that the Spanish nation has declared herself—true to her historical noble character—to be, as it were, an asylum for the persons and the property of foreigners, whether Americans or Chinese, residing within the limits of her dominions.

How can the advocate, whom the government of that noble nation has happened to select to be her advocate before the commission of arbitration, dare say in presence of that law, that it was rightful for the authorities of Cuba to place embargoes upon the property of American citizens in that island?

Here is the text in full of the said law:

*Ley de 28 de Setiembre de 1820.*

ARTICULO 1°. El territorio español es un asilo inviolable para las personas y propiedades pertenecientes á extrangeros, *sea que estos residan en España ó fuera de ella,* con tal que respeten la constitucion y demas leyes que gobiernan.

ART. 2°. El asilo de las personas se entiende sin perjuicio de los tratados existentes con otras potencias; y mediante que en estos no pueden considerarse comprendidas las opiniones políticas, se declara, que los perseguidos por ellas, que residan en España, no serán entregados por el gobierno, si no son reos de alguno de los delitos expresados en dichos tratados.

ART. 3°. Los individuos comprendidos en el artículo anterios y sus propiedades gozarán de la misma proteccion, que las leyes dispensan á las de los españoles.

ART. 4°. Ni á titulo de represalias en tiempo de guerra, ni por otro ningun motivo, podrán confiscarse, secuestrarse, ni embargarse dichas propiedades ; á no ser las que pertenezcan á los gobiernos que se hallen en guerra con la nacion española, ó á sus auxiliares.

I think it useful to give here the translation of this statute :

"ART. 1st. The Spanish territory is an inviolable asylum for the persons and for the property of foreigners, *both when these foreigners reside in Spain and when they live outside of her dominions ;* provided, however, that they respect the constitution and the laws of the country.

"ART. 2d. This asylum, as far as the persons is concerned, shall be without prejudice to the treaty stipulations already made with other powers; but as in these stipulations the offenses of a political character cannot be spoken of, it is hereby enacted that no foreigners residing in Spain shall be delivered to their respective government, and that their political offenses shall not be considered comprehended among the crimes mentioned in the above-named treaties.

"ART. 3d. The persons spoken of in the foregoing treaty, as well as their property, shall enjoy exactly the same protection as the persons and property of Spaniards.

"ART. 4th. Not even as reprisals in time of war, nor for any other reason whatever shall it be lawful to *confiscate, sequestrate,* or *embargo* the said property ; but it shall be lawful to do so when the property belongs either to the governments with which the Spanish nation is at war, or to their allies or auxiliaries."

This seems to be plain enough. *Confiscar, secuestrar, embargar.* It looks as if the Spanish legislator foresaw the contingency, now realized, that a foreigner, to whom the language of Spain is unknown, would try to torture the meaning of the word "*embargo*" with the assistance of the worst English and Spanish dictionary ever made in the world.

The authorities of Cuba were forbidden by statute to confiscate, sequestrate, or embargo the property of all foreigners, neither as reprisals in times of war, nor for any other reason whatever.

But there is another law which the advocate for Spain may find if he wishes to increase his learning, in the *coleccion legislativa de España,* year 1855, or if he does not wish to hunt it up there, in the most handy *Diccionario de Legislacion,* by Sanguineti, vol. 3d, page 846. Both works are in the law library at the Capitol.

This law was enacted on the 4th of December, 1845, and contains the following provision :

" No podrán confiscarse las propriedades de los extrangeros, ni aun en el caso de hallarse España en guerra con la nacion á que estos corresponden."

Or in English:

" The property of foreigners shall never be confiscated, even in case Spain is at war with the nation to which they belong."

What then about the " rightfulness of the embargo of the property of American citizens in Cuba ? "

The history of these " *embargoes,*" which the advocate of Spain attempts to prove to be rightful, forms one of the most shameful features of the system adopted by the Spanish authorities of Cuba (not by Spain) to put down the insurrection. In fact, the system was invented alone to foment corruption, to enable men, both in public and private positions, to grow rich in a short time, and to corrupt to the very core all seeds of morality which might remain in the administration of the government there.

The first idea of seizing the property of all persons in sympathy with

12

the rebellion, as a means of retaliation, and for the purpose of distributing it among the "loyalists" (*los leales*), appeared in the mouth of March, 1869, in the shape of a private communication to the editor of the newspaper named *Prensa de la Habana*. On the following day an editorial, signed by Don José Ruiz de Leon, appeared in the *Diario de la Marina*, advocating the same idea, and urging the government to adopt that measure.

General Dulce, the governor-general of Cuba at that time, a man of indomitable courage, a profound diplomatist, and a generous, good-hearted governor, resisted as much as he could putting his signature to a decree which he himself used to name a "*barbaridad*," a barbarous action. He succeeded in putting off this matter until the 1st of April, at which date he signed the first decree ever issued upon this matter; but even then he managed in such a way as to hold it back until the 16th of April, when at last it was given to the public in the Gaceta of that day.

So it appears from the preamble of the circular of April 20, in the second paragraph of which (see p. 73 of the advocate of Spain's pamphlet) it is said:

"You will have likewise become acquainted with my decree of the 1st instant published in the *Gaceta* of *the 16th*," &c.

And so it is known by everybody who knows anything about the history of those calamitous times.

General Dulce could resist no longer, in spite of his great qualities above spoken of, because he had no forces to oppose the rabid bands of volunteers who besieged his palace, and who on the 2d of June invaded it, and compelled him to resign his office into the hands of General Espinar, at the time the favorite of that rabble.

If the advocate for Spain wishes to be informed about the pressure exercised on General Dulce by the volunteers and the subaltern authorities, all of them conspiring against him, he will do well to read the two reports made by General Dulce to the supreme government of Madrid, dated the one on board the steamer Guipuzcoa on the 18th of June, 1869, and the other in Madrid on the 2d of July of the same year. He will find both documents in the book entitled, "CUBA: ESTUDIOS POLITICOS," published in Madrid, with the approval of the government, by DonCarlos de Sedano, now the Count of Casa Sedano.

But be it as it may, there is no doubt that the decrees of April 1869, permitting embargoes to be placed upon the property of all persons suspected to be in sympathy with the insurrection, regulating the management of that property and creating a council, to have charge of the administration of this property and all matters connected with it, became a law in Cuba and that *bongré malgré* they were carried into effect.

The advocate for Spain is mistaken in saying (chapter VI. of his pamphlet, headed "*Spanish decrees*") that those decrees were three, because there were five; and he is mistaken also in stating that they read as he says.

Those five decrees, dated respectively, one on the 1st of April, another on the 15th, two others on the 17th, and the last one on the 20th (all in April, 1869), were translated into English and published in New York in pamphlet form, under the title of "*circulars and decrees of the Captain General of the Island of Cuba, for the embargo of property and the annihilation of civil rights in 1869*." This pamphlet has been put on file in various cases before the commission; among others, in the case No. 29, of Ramon Fernandez Criado y Gomez; and a copy of it is also appended to these " remarks," as note No. 6.

The same decrees were translated into English by the United States consul general at Havana, Mr. Plumb, and sent by him to the Secretary of State, who in his turn submitted them to Congress. They were printed in executive document No. 108, Senate, forty-first Congress, second session, being a " message of the President of the United States, on seizure of American vessels, and injuries to American citizens in Cuba," pages 226, 227, 228, and 229.

The same decrees as written in Spanish are before this commission in the official book published in Havana, in 1870, under the title " *Datos y noticias oficiales sobre los bienes mandados embargar por disposicion gubernativa*," a copy of which forms part of the record of the case No. 48, of Antonio Máximo Mora *vs.* Spain.

It will be seen hereafter that no one of these decrees speaks a word about courts, or judicial proceedings against the persons deprived of their property, as the advocate for Spain supposes. The necessities of methodical exposition require me to postpone this part of the subject.

The enormity of the sin committed by the creating of such *executive embargoes*, perceived from the very first moment by General Dulce, from whom they were extorted by force, was not less noticed by his successors.

General Espinar, in whose hands General Dulce was forced to resign his authority, went away, and General Caballero de Rodas came to occupy his place as governor general of Cuba. He saw the " *irregularity*" of the embargoes, and for this very reason he issued in September of the same year, 1869, an order the text of which is appended to these " remarks," as note No. 7, by which he instructed Don Francisco Montaos y Rovillar to act as judge advocate, and institute legal proceedings against the persons supposed to be connected with the revolution.

This decree, intended to regulate the order of things created under the decrees of General Dulce, and to turn the *executive embargoes*, first, into *judicial embargoes* by order and authority of law, and then into *final confiscation*, did not reach any practical result, except as to the property of 52 persons, who were the only ones prosecuted under it. It did not stop the evil, which soon increased to such an extent that at the end of 1870 the property of more than TEN THOUSAND PEOPLE had already been seized *without judicial action and merely by executive order of a purely political character*. The " *Datos y noticias oficiales*," above referred to, contain the list of the persons so deprived of their property up to the time of its publication (1870).

The government itself did not know what to do with the great number of plantations, farms, and estates of all kinds, houses, &c., &c., accumulated in its hands ; and the administration of this immense amount of property, of which the government was merely a trustee, gave rise to a system of robbery and corruption never equaled in history.

The *Datos y noticias oficiales* contain a report, in which it is said that the administrators appointed to manage the sugar plantations appeared to think that they were enjoying *prebendas ó canonicatos*, ecclesiastical benefices, and not managing the property of others (page    of this pamphlet).

General Caballero de Rodas made, it is true, the first attempt to improve this matter, but he did not go any further. The volunteers were too strong at that time ; and the governor-general of Cuba, even if he

14

had had any desire to do otherwise, was compelled to temporize with
them and leave their favorite communistic scheme to go on unchanged.
The pressure of that organization, as remarkable in Cuban history as
that of the Pretorians in Rome or the Janissaries in Turkey, was such as
at that time to have compelled this very Captain-General De Rodas to
sign and publish in the Gaceta the decree, which I appended to these
" remarks," as note No. 8, by which he condemned to imprisonment all
the members of a council of war, because the decision of that court was
deemed to be too lenient!

General Cabellero de Rodas became, at last, so unpopular with the
volunteers that he had to resign. The height of his unpopularity was
reached when he put in prison the editor of *El Cronista*, a rabid Spanish paper published in New York, who had gone to Cuba to create
there, personally, the same agitation he was fomenting here. ·

Then General Valmaseda became the governor-general of Cuba; and
although he was a saint of the volunteers' devotion, he could not bear
the arrogant tone and the peculiar dictatorial ways of the council of
administration of embargoed property, and he abolished it. (See note
No. 9.)

Time passed away and brought its usual softening and smoothing of
all things. King Amadeo ascended the throne of Spain and issued his
celebrated decree of the 6th August, 1872. (See note No. 10.)

That king established the *junta de la deuda*, and ordered a general
revision of all the cases of *embargo*, and a division of them into two
classes—one comprising those in which there were some proofs against
the party whose property was seized ; the other for the cases in which
there were no proofs. The cases of the first class were directed to be
sent immediately to the courts of justice. In the cases of the second
class, the property was ordered to be released at once.

This decree obtained scarcely any attention at all in the island of
Cuba. The junta de la deuda was no better than the old council.
(See note No. 11.)

Then the republic was established in Spain. The embargoes were
abolished (see note No. 12); the ministro de ultramar came to Cuba
to enforce the decree, but the volunteers and the " CASINO," which was
then the real Government of Cuba, answered by another decree putting
up to sale the property, and causing the ministro to go back to Spain.
(See notes 12 and 13.)

These *embargoes*, which from the very beginning always exhibited a
socialistic character, and were the delight of the rabble and of the government employes, could not be abolished in full until Marshal Martinez Campos came to Cuba with twenty-six thousand regular troops, and
put the volunteers under control. (See note No. 14.)

It has been seen, very plainly, I think, that the "executive embargoes," from General Dulce to Marshal Martinez Campos, were always
the subject of two different streams of opinion—one of constant hate and
animadversion on the part of the authorities in Spain; another of constant love on the part of the mob. The latter manifested itself in various
ways by repeated acts of defiance to the legitimate authority ; while the
former found eloquent expression in the steps successively taken to
counteract the tendency of the *embargoes* until they were reduced to
nothing.

It was reserved for the advocate for Spain, in Washington, to attempt
the justification of a measure which has found its strongest condemnation in the words of Spain herself.

Don Práxedes Mateo Sagasta, secretary of state, in Madrid, in 1870, told General Sickles that "*embargoes in Cuba had been only a purely political measure,*" and that they were not "*based upon any law which ordains sequestration of property.*" (Note of September 2, 1870.)

The President of the Republic of Spain, Don Francisco Pi y Margall, in his decree of July 12, 1873, said:

"In consideration of the representations set forth by the minister of the colonies, the government of the republic decrees the following:

"ART. 1st. All embargoes put upon the property of infidentes BY EX-ECUTIVE ORDER, in consequence of the decree of April 20, 1869, are declared to be removed from the date in which the present decree, published in the Gaceta de Madrid, shall reach the capital of the island of Cuba."

And the representations set forth by the minister of the colonies, upon which the President of the Republic removed all embargoes placed *executively*, under the decree of April, 1869, upon the property of persons deemed to be *infidentes*, are the ones contained in the preamble of the decree, or, as the advocate for Spain calls it, the report of Don Francisco Suñer y Capdevila.

To this decree of July 12, 1873, the advocate for Spain has devoted the XXII chapter of his pamphlet, from page 59 to page 68. He has made a desperate attempt to make two things out of the decree and separate its *preámbulo* or *parte explicativa* from the articles, or *parte dispositiva*, by stating that although the condemnation of the *embargoes* is in the said "*preámbulo*," it is not found, however, in the decree itself. *The decree itself*, he says, *can have no bearing upon the question of the rightfulness of the embargoes.*"

It was issued upon the representations made in the *preámbulo*; it abolished the *embargoes* in consequence of the said representations; and it has "*no bearing upon the question of the rightfulness of the embargoes*"!!!

Then the advocate for Spain is bold enough to exclaim:

"What importance should be attached to the utterances, opinions, or measures of a minister elevated for a moment to office by political convulsion, and in another moment swept into obscurity? How could be, by his opinions, commit Spain to a future course of conduct, or determine for Spain which course was not lawful or proper?"

And then he quotes from Mr. Cushing, and says that in Spain, "liberals, radicals, republicans, and constitutionals, do not possess *discretion* (and he italicizes this word), and do not do anything *practicable* (and he italicizes also the word "practicable"), and set forth only "*extravagant doctrines*" of "*impossible application*"! (The italics are also his.)

I will say nothing else in this respect, except that when the advocate for Spain was in the pay of the republic, or in the pay of the Sagasta ministry, *liberal*, the one which has now succeeded to Cánovas del Castillo, and of the other "radicals," and "constitutionals," who ruled Spain from 1869 to 1875, he did not deem them to be indiscreet, extravagant, and impracticable.

But the government which ordered the property of Antonio Maximo Mora, and Ramon Fernandez Criádo y Gomez, was the government of the present King Alfonso XII.

The advocate for Spain devotes his Chapter VI, page 13, to what he calls *Spanish decrees*, and says that "in April, 1869, in the seventh month of the contest above described, the authorities of Spain in Cuba directed the institution of JUDICIAL PROCEEDINGS against the property of persons charged with complicity in the insurrection, *and three decrees were issued in that month prescribing the course* of proceeding." He ap-

pended to his pamphlet one of these three decrees, dated April 17, page
71, another of the same date, page 72, and the well known circular of
April 20, 1869, page 73.

Then he gives what he calls the main features of the decrees, and
adds:

"It will be observed that the question of the guilt or innocence of the
accused was not to be decided by the board which was charged with the
care of embargoed property. *That question was to be determined in other
proceedings before courts-martial.*"

"The proceedings of these courts," he says further, "were so conducted
as to allow the defendants every proper opportunity of defense in person
or by counsel. It appears from records in several cases before this
Commission, that notice was given by publication to the defendants to
appear, and in case of non appearance judgment of condemnation was
given by default."

Nothing of all this is true.

The ideas of the advocate for Spain about this matter are fearfully
mixed up.

The decrees of April, 1869, never directed *the institution of judicial
proceedings*, nor did they *prescribe the course of such proceedings*.

Read the first one of April 17, in page 71 of the pamphlet of the advocate
of Spain. It establishes the council of administration of embargoed property; it says who are to be members thereof; it provides that the funds
raised by these embargoes shall be deposited in the Treasury; it gives authority to the council *to decide all doubtful matters*; and "*those only of a
judicial or legal nature* shall be brought TO ME for decision." TO ME
means the Governor General, not the courts. It determines the powers of the lieutenant governor of the island; and it commands the council to suggest the reforms which in the course of time it might find
necessary.

Not a single word about courts, or courts-martial, or judicial proceedings.

In the other decree of the same date (page 72) the same thing occurs.
It merely provides for the appointment of president and members of the
council.

The third decree, that is the circular of April 20 (page 73, and the
following), contains 34 articles, none of which speaks of judicial proceedings or courts martial, or courts of any kind to investigate the guilt
of the parties whose property was *embargoed*.

On the contrary, article 6, page 74, provides for an investigation to
be made at once by the governors and lieutenant-governors, and orders
that this investigation must be "*gubernativa*," or "executive," or "government investigation," and not judicial.

Article 8 (page 75) repeats that the investigation must be "*governmental*," and prescribes the record thereof to be sent to the council of
administration of embargoed property.

Where, therefore, has the advocate for Spain read in these decrees
*that the question of the guilt or innocence of the accused was not to be de-
cided by the board, but was to be determined in other proceedings before court
martials?*

Will he be kind enough to point out any passage in any of the decrees
of April, 1869, stating what he says?

It will be in vain. No such thing exists nor was thought of at that
time. All that the learned counsel of the other side says about this
point is pure imagination, *ægri somnia*, and nothing else.

Under these decrees of April, 1869, no opportunity of defense was given the owners of the property embargoed. In being deprived of their property by these *embargoes*, they became *ipso facto* deprived of their civil rights (article 3d). They could not appear before any court either in person or by attorney. The attorneys and agents that the parties had in Cuba ceased to be such from the date of the embargo, and the government appointed a new one, as it did in the case of Cristobal Madan, or did not appoint any at all.

When inquiries were made about this matter, the political secretary informed Mr. Plumb that persons intending to prove their innocence in regard to this matter had to appear before the Spanish consul of the place where they were residing, and file with him testimony of trustworthy persons, said testimony to be transmitted to the captain-general (not to any court), who would repeal the embargo if the testimony was satisfactory to him. (See dispatch of Mr. Plumb to Mr. Davis, August 25, 1869, note No. 15.)

So the estates of Ramon de Rivas y Lamar, and many others, were released.

The advocate for Spain is mistaken in saying that the records of the commission show what he says. This is not true.

Out of the 135 cases on the docket of this commission there are only four in which there have been proceedings before a court martial, and proclamations, and opportunity for defense. These cases are the cases of Francisco Cr. Yzquierdo, No. 7; Joaquin M. Delgado, No. 31; Ramon Fernandez Criado, No. 29; and Antonio Maximo Mora, No. 48. None of the others present the features which the advocate for Spain wishes to give them.

It may be added, for the edification of the advocate for Spain, that the so called judicial proceedings against those four persons were annulled by His Majesty the present King of Spain, and that the property of those parties was ordered to be restored to them.

It is under this very erroneous idea that, in his Chapter VII, page 15, headed with the phrase "*Objections to embargoes*," the advocate for Spain also says, as follows:

"It has been objected to these embargoes that so far as they affected American citizens they violated the treaty of 1795, *because* (mark this) proceedings were taken in the absence of the interested parties, and not conducted before the ordinary judicial tribunals, and also that cognizance was taken of acts committed by American citizens beyond the territorial jurisdiction of Spain, and even in the United States."

Nothing of this was done under the decrees of April, 1869; and the objections made to the executive *embargoes* provided *by* those decrees were other and very different objections than those supposed by the advocate for Spain. The objections spoken of by him were raised afterwards, in November, 1870, and not against the *embargoes*, but against the decision of the council of war which met at Havana, on the 7th of that month and year, and condemned to death and confiscation of property fifty-two persons in a lump.

The umpire, who certainly will not allow himself to be led astray by the anachronisms and sophistical argumentation of the advocate for Spain, will find very easily, by perusing the correspondence between General Sickles and Don Praxides Mateo Sagasta and Don Cristino Martos, Spanish secretaries of state, both of them, and between Mr. Fish and Don Mauricio Lopez Roberts, Admiral Polo de Bernabé, and Don Antonio Mantilla, that the objections raised against the embargoes were founded on the extraordinary character of the measure, on its unlawfulness according to the laws of Spain, and on its being at variance with

2 SP

and in full violation of the treaty stipulations of 1795, not *because proceedings were taken in the absence of the interested parties*, &c., as supposed, but because the *embargoes* were forbidden by the treaty, and because nothing can be done against American citizens in Spain, according to the same treaty, unless by *authority of law only*, and not by executive decrees which *have no foundation of law* at all, as acknowledged by Señor Sagasta.

The first word ever uttered against judicial proceedings against absent Americans, &c., is to be found in the note of Mr. Fish to General Sickles, dated November 25, 1870.

The advocate for Spain devotes the Chapter XVIII of his pamphlet, headed "*Treaty of* 1795," to prove that these "*embargoes*" of property by executive decree of the governors-general of Cuba were not forbidden by the VIIth article of that treaty. He travels from the English and Spanish Dictionary of Newman and Barretti to the Encyclopedia Britannica; he speaks of the *Jus Angeriæ* in his XIXth chapter, page 50; he writes another chapter (the XXth), which he heads "*The treaty further discussed*"; and he concludes, after a great display of erudition, that the embargoes are lawful under the treaty.

This idea was first broached in Spain by Don Praxedes Matea Sagasta, but was abandoned by him and his successor, Mr. Martos, and up to this time, including the Spanish ministers here, and also the authorities of Cuba, no one has ever construed the treaty in the way now set forth by the advocate of Spain.

No American official has understood it in that way.

No member of this commission did ever entertain such views.

No umpire has had them for a moment in his mind.

The present advocate for Spain has the glory to have set it forth for the first time in the eleventh year of the existence of this commission. *Tardio, pero seguro!*

The question has always been whether the man was or was not an American citizen. If he was such a citizen of the United States, nobody doubted that the embargo was unlawful, and that the property should be restored.

The Spanish arbitrator himself agreed to this point in the case of Gonzaly Poey, No. 66, and in others. He never construed the treaty as the advocate of Spain finds now advisable to construe it. He himself did not think in this way some months ago. In the case of Felix Govin y Pinto, No. 9, which was a case of embargo of property, he commenced his own brief by saying that claimant would be entitled to have his money restored to him if he were a citizen of the United States.

Chapter VIII of the pamphlet, beginning page 16, and headed "*Legislation of the United States*," seeks to justify the executive embargoes decreed in Cuba, because in the United States the estate and property of certain persons were seized and confiscated during the civil war from 1861 to 1865. And in order to meet the objection that the civil war was a "war," while the insurrection of Cuba never "assumed the conditions which amount to a war," as President Grant said in his special message to Congress of June 13, 1870, which impeded the recognition of belligerency, and as every Spanish official always maintained, he wrote his Chapter IX, "*The contest in Cuba a war*," page 19; his Chapter X, "*Cuban insurgents not recognized as belligerents by the United States*," page 21; and his Chapter XI, headed "*War a fact*," page 25; and concluded by saying (page 27) that "the actual existence of war was as much matter of fact in Cuba, in 1869, as in the Southern States in 1861; and

19

that whatever justification the United States had for the acts by which they crippled their insurgents, Spain had for the decrees of embargo."

All of this might be very good, if the purpose of the advocate for Spain were to prove the righteousness of the embargo of the property of Spanish subjects. What the United States did with their revolted citizens might or might not justify, perhaps, what Spain did with her revolted subjects. But the pamphlet of the advocate for Spain is intended to prove " *the rightfulness of the embargo of the property of* AMERICAN CITIZENS," and not of Spanish subjects, in the island of Cuba.

If any argument drawn from similarity is to be admitted in questions of *rightfulness*, the advocate for Spain would have to prove that the United States seized and confiscated lawfully the property of foreign subjects in the United States. But he cannot prove nor attempt to prove such a thing, first, because his arguments would not be founded on truth; and, second, because by so doing he would fatally injure the Spanish claims against the United States which the late Spanish premier, Don Antonio Cánovas del Castillo, wishes to urge against the American government (see note of Mr. Cushing to Mr. Evarts dated March 30, 1877, in page 497, Foreign Relations of the United States in 1877). One of those claims, specially the claim for the seizure of the steamer *Nuestra Señora de Regla*, presently pressed by the Spanish minister, Don Felipe Mendez De Vigo, would fall to the ground.

No. The criterion of Spain, whatever right or wrong in dealing with her subjects, could not be the criterion applicable to her dealing with American citizens. The advocate for Spain may glorify what Spain did with Cuba, which every honest Spaniard thinks to have been shameful robbery; but he cannot say that American citizens, foreigners to Spain, were liable to see themselves deprived of their property by executive decrees, or by any decrees of any kind at all, because, in the first place, there is the VIIth article of the treaty between the United States and Spain of 1795, and because, in the second place, there are the laws of 1820, which I have copied in the beginning of these "remarks," by which all sequestrations, embargoes, and confiscations of property were forbidden, even in times of war, and as a means of retaliation.

The XIIIth chapter of the pamphlet entitled " *The tribunals in Cuba,*" page 30, rests exclusively upon the error that the *embargoes*, under the circular of April 20, 1869, had anything to do with the court-martial against whose proceedings Secretary Fish protested in November, 1870.

We have proved that out of all the cases before this commission there are only four, in which the guilt of the parties was subjected to *judicial* investigation (see note No. 18); and that consequently the great number of cases (many of which are already decided) arising out of *mere executive embargoes* under the decrees of April 1869 can find no justification in the supposed action of courts which never existed except in the imagination of the advocate for Spain.

The tribunals in Cuba at that time were about as much tribunals as the revolutionary tribunals of France in 1793. Is the advocate for Spain unaware that the court rooms were always invaded and occupied to the fullness of their capacity by armed bands of volunteers? If he is willing in good faith to know the truth about it, he may ask Don Antonio Batanero how things happened with him when he sat to try Leon and Medina, Cabias and Mrs. Rosanis, in March, 1869.

Does he not know that the terror prevailed to such an extent among the judges that the chief justice of the Audiencia, an exceptional truly honest man, deemed it necessary to issue his circular of January 27, 1869 (see note No. 19), recommending the judges to show civic courage, and not yield to pressure?

Has he forgotten that when forty medical students were submitted to trial the court room was surrounded by several thousand volunteers in arms, with their chiefs at their head? That when two sentences were passed which did not meet the approval of the besieging forces, it was at last necessary, in order to appease their fury, to render a third judgment, by which eight of those children were sentenced to death, and the balance of thirty-two sent to *presidio* (hard labor) in the streets of of Havana?

For these iniquities, perhaps applauded by the advocate of Spain, but looked at with horror by every Spaniard in the world, even those who executed them, it was that the agreement of February 12, 1871, gave this commission the power to review the adjudications made by those tribunals. They were not tribunals; they lacked sanctity and independence; they were a real mockery, miserable tools in the hands of the enraged mob.

Now, I will say a word about the court-martial of November 7, 1870.

The commission is indebted to the advocate for Spain for a full knowledge of its proceedings.

I had asked, through you, different portions of the record of that celebrated trial; but, as usual, what was sent in answer to our call was incomplete, or encumbered with other matters.

But the advocate for Spain wanted to have this record, because it served his purposes in one case, and he, of course, succeeded in obtaining it in full. It is on file as defensive evidence in the case of Ramon Fernandez Criado y Gomez *vs.* Spain, No. 29.

This record shows, page 54 of that evidence, that on the 12th of October, 1870, some days before the sentence was passed, the judge-advocate sent a communication to the captain-general of Cuba, stating that against Ramon Fernandez Criado y Gomez and three other people there were no proofs, and suggesting that his name and the names of the other three should be withdrawn from the case, at least for the moment.

The captain-general consulted upon the matter with the *Auditor de guerra*, who is his legal adviser in matters of military law; and, upon his advice, refused to comply with the suggestion of the judge-advocate, and ordered sentence to be passed.

The ground of this decision was that, as the proceedings were in *rebeldia*, by default, and as the sentence, whatever it might be, could not be executed until the parties were arrested, in which case the proceedings had to be commenced *a novo*, it mattered little what the sentence decided.

Upon this consideration the council of war met on the 7th of November, 1870, and condemned that very same man, Ramon Fernandez Criado y Gomez, against whom no proofs had been found, to death and confiscation of property. Pontius Pilate acted better than these gentlemen. He at least washed his hands.

In the record of these proceedings, page 48, it appears also that Antonio Maximo Mora had never been a member of the "Cuban junta," and nevertheless he was also condemned, as such, to death and confiscation.

So it was, that when Mr. Cushing called the attention of the Count of Casa Valencia, then the Spanish secretary of state, and his successor, Don Fernando Calderon y Collantes, to all these iniquities, the result was the one we know.

The sentence, as far as Ramon Fernandez Criado, Antonio Maximo Mora, and Joaquin Delgado, was annulled, in the only way in which sentences can be annulled in Spain, by means of an *indulto*, and the property of these three persons was ordered to be restored to them.

A fourth person, Francisco C. Yzquieido, was subsequently added to that list.

All of this is well known in the commission. The diplomatic correspondence referred to is on file (see note No. 20). The decision of the King is also on file. And everybody knows also how desperate are the efforts of the advocate for Spain to counteract that royal decision, and leave the property of these Americans in the hands of the Spanish authorities of Cuba.

In Chapter XIV, entitled " *Practice of the United States justified,*" the Government of the United States is administered a grain of comfort, by the approval of their confiscation law by the advocate for Spain. He is generous enough to continue his work of mercy by proving in his XVth chapter, headed " SELF-*defense*," page 33, that " self-defense is part of the law of our nature," and other reasonings of this kind.

It is a pity that he had forgotten that self-defense has to be JUST, and that when it is not *just* and *proportionate* to the attack, ceases to be right, and becomes as wrong as all other wrongs. If the theory of the enlightened lawyer, author of the pamphlet which is the subject of these " remarks," were to be followed, the thief who robs a thief would be justifiable.

Chapter XVI, page 36, headed *Precautionary seizures*, is intended to prove that the " embargoes" could be made lawfully, without proofs, and even without suspicion of the guilt. The principle of the advocate for Spain is the following (page 36):

" To justify seizures it is not always necessary that there should be suspicion of actual guilt. The existence of danger may justify a seizure under circumstances which, in the absence of danger, would not warrant it."

This doctrine goes side by side by the other one maintained by him in the Juan San Pedro's case, when he said that if for the arrest of a man proofs were necessary few men would be arrested.

Unfortunately for the advocate for Spain, the law foresaw that such an argument might be used in the future by some lawyer, ready to defend all causes, as the minister without portfolio in the celebrated book of Laboulaye, *Le Prince Caniche.*

The law reads:

" *Ni á titulo de represalias en* tiempo de guerra, ni por ningun otro motivo, podrán confiscarse, secuestrarse, ni embargarse dichas propiedades, á no ser las que pertenezcan á los gobiernos, que se hallen en guerra con la nacion española, y á sus auxiliares.

" No podrán confiscarse las propiedades de los extraugeros, ni aun en el caso de hallarse España en guerra con la nacion á que estos correspondan."

Therefore, no possible justification can be found for these seizures, neither in the fact (if so it is the fact) that the United States resorted to it nor in any consideration of self-defense.

Seizures of the property of foreigners are impossible in Spain; and no reason of any kind can be set forth to justify them.

Chapter XVII, " *Vindication of the embargoes,*" page 40, and Chapter XXI, " *Self-defense and treaty stipulations,*" page 57, in which the author of the pamphlet introduces the idea that treaty stipulations can be overridden when the necessities of self-defense require it are already answered. Both chapters fall to the ground under the broad terms of the laws of 1820.

The easy morality of Chapter XXI is worthy to be noticed. Of course, the one who measures the extent and the necessity of self-defense as he has done is the same who is capable of violating the treaty. What would be in this case the binding force of the international agreements? It is to be hoped that the learned author of the pamphlet will never occupy any diplomatic position, nor be at the head of the State Department either here or in Spain.

## Recapitulation.

1. In Spain no other *embargoes* of property than the one decreed by the courts of justice, both in civil and criminal cases, are known. (See Escriche Diccionario ; word *embargo*.)

2. No embargoes can be placed upon private property by executive decree.

3. Out of the 135 claimants before this commission there has been only four claimants against whose property a judicial embargo was placed, and this was in September 9, 1870. (See pages, 53 and 54 of evidence for Spain, in the case of Ramon Fernandez Criado y Gomez, No. 29.) These four cases are the cases of Francisco C. Yzquierdo, Ramon Fernandez Criado y Gomez, Joaquin M. Delgado, and Antonio Máximo Mora, they were all American citizens at that time.

4. The embargoes under the decrees of April, 1869, were political measures, intended for political purposes, and the tribunals had nothing to do with them.

5. According to the laws of Spain the property of all foreigners, Swedes and Americans and Russians, cannot be embargoed, sequestrated, or confiscated, for any reason at all, even in times of war, by means of reprisals.

6. The Cuban embargoes were repealed as illegal in 1873, and the repeal was never disapproved by the government which succeeded the republic.

7. The embargo and the confiscation of the property of American citizens in Cuba, even by reason of self-defense, were forbidden by the laws above recited, and by the treaty of 1795 between the United States and Spain.

8. Spain has canceled the restoration of the property of the American citizens so seized, embargoed, and confiscated. The republican government ordered the release of the property of the persons named in the telegram of November 7, 1873. His Majesty, the King Alfonso XII, has ordered the restoration of the property of Antonio Máximo Mora, Magdalene Farres de Mora, his wife, and Ramon Fernandez Criado y Gomez.

9. Neither the arbitrators nor the umpires have ever held that the *embargoes* were rightful, and on the contrary the heavy awards made in favor of Angarica, Delgado, Poey, Youngs, Smith & Co., and others, have shown their indisposition to accept the doctrine now set forth for the first time by the advocate for Spain.

I am, respectfully yours,

J. I. RODRIGUEZ.

23

NOTE No. 1.

Secretary Fish, in his communication of the 18th of April, 1874, addressed to Admiral Polo de Bernabé, used the following language:

"The insurrection which broke out at Yara, in the autumn of 1868, has had the unusual good fortune of having the justice of the complaints which it alleges in its justification recognized by those who are engaged in suppressing it. On the 10th of September, 1869, the minister of transmarine affairs, at Madrid, in an official paper, said:

"A deplorable and pertinacious tradition of despotism, which, if it could ever be justified, is without a shadow of reason at the present time, intrusted the direction and management of our colonial establishments to the agents of the metropolis, destroying by their dominant and exclusive authority the vital energies of the country and the creative and productive activity of free individuals. And although the system may now have improved in some of its details, the domineering action of the authorities being less felt, it still appears full of the original error, which is upheld by the force of tradition, and the necessary influence of interests created under their protection, which, doubtless, are deserving of respect, so far as they are reconcilable with the requirements of justice, with the common welfare, and with the principles on which every liberal system should be founded. A change of system, political as well as administrative, is therefore imperitively demanded." (Executive DOCUMENT B, Senate, special session, being a "message of the President, with regard to the claim of indemnity from Spain for the execution at Santiago de Cuba of persons who were on board the Virginius," pages 45 and 46.)

General Don Domingo Dulce, in the report submitted by him in January, 1867, to the colonial secretary, expressed himself as follows:

"Los insulares, y muchos de los peninsulares allí arraigados, aspiran á la asimilacion con la madre patria . . . aspiran á ser españoles, porque entienden que el estado en que se encuentran hace mas de treinta años, implica una especie de extrañamiento, ó expulsion de la gran familia á que pertenecen; consideran, pues, la cuestion de esos derechos, no solo bajo el aspecto de su conveniencia, sino tambien y principalmente bajo el de su dignidad, y es bien sabido lo que consideraciones de esa especie pueden en el ánimo y en el corazon de los hombres de raza española." (Informacion sobre reformas en Cuba y Puerto Rico; Tomo I, page, 224.)

Marshal Serrano, subsequently the regent of the kingdom of Spain, gave also his report on the same subject. It bears the date of May 10, 1867. Among other passages of this important document, I select the following:

"Yo no he podido ménos de reconocer, no puedo ménos de decir hoy al gobierno de S. M., con la lealtad de mi carácter, y á impulso del mas íntimo convencimiento, que LAS QUEJAS DE LOS CUBANOS SON JUSTAS, que sus aspiraciones son legítimas, que no hay razon para que ellos, españoles como nosotros, no tengan prensa, ni representacion ninguna en su gobierno, ni una sola de las garantias constitucionales á que en la península tenemos derecho; que no hay razon ninguna para que un gobierno militar y absoluto, desde los mas altos hasta lo mas bajos grados de la escala, sea el único régimen de las Antillas." (Informacion sobre reformas en Cuba y Puerto Rico, Tomo II, page, 192.)

## Note No. 2.

### Count Valmaseda's Proclamation.

Inhabitants of the country! The re-enforcements of troops that I have been waiting for have arrived; with them I shall give protection to the good, and punish promptly those that still remain in rebellion against the government of the metropolis.

You know that I have pardoned those that have fought us with arms; that your wives, mothers, and sisters have found in me the unexpected protection that you have refused them. You know, also, that many of those I have pardoned have turned against us again.

Before such ingratitude, such villainy, it is not possible for me to be the man that I have been; there is no longer a place for a falsified neutrality; be that is not for me is against me, and that my soldiers may know how to distinguish, you bear the order they carry:

1st. Every man, from the age of fifteen years, upward, found away from his habitation (finca), and does not prove a justified motive therefor, will be shot.

2d. Every habitation unoccupied will be burned by the troops.

3d. Every habitation from which does not float a white flag, as a signal that its occupants desire peace, will be reduced to ashes.

Women that are not living at their own homes, or at the house of their relatives, will collect in the town of Jiguani, or Bayamo, where maintenance will be provided. Those who do not present themselves will be conducted forcibly.

The foregoing determinations will commence to take effect on the 14th of the present month.

EL CONDE DE VALMASEDA.

Bayamo, *April* 4, 1869.

## Note No. 3.

See proclamation by the President of the United States of America, of October 12, 1870, in page XIV of the Appendix to vol. 16 of the United States Statutes at Large.

See, also, note of Mr. Fish to General Sickles, November 25, 1870:

"The revolutionary body known as the Cuban Junta VOLUNTARILY DISBANDED ITSELF ABOUT ONE MONTH AGO, and announced its intention to discontinue any hostile purpose it might have entertained against Spanish rule in Cuba. During its previous history its acts, so far as conflicting with the laws of the United States and the international duties of this government, were repressed by the President." (Papers relating to the foreign affairs of the United States in 1870, pages 220 and 221.)

## Note No. 4.

General Don Nicolas de Mahy, governor general of Cuba, in a report given by him to the King, on the 12th of September, 1821, said the following:

"Ojalá que no hubiese sino cubanos: en tal caso bien se podria re] sponder hasta con la vida de la incontrastable adhesion de este isla a

gobierno español." (Vida de Don José de la Luz y Caballero, por José Ignacio Rodrigues; 2nd edition, page 15.)
The island was given the title of *ever faithful*, which she retained until 1868.

---

## Note No. 5.

The words of General Dulce, about the wrongs done to the Cubans, must be repeated here:

"Consideran la cuestion de esos derechos no solo bajo el aspecto de su conveniencia, sino tambien y *principalmente* bajo el de su dignidad, y es bien sabido lo que consideraciones de esa especie pueden en el ánimo y en el corazon de los hombres de raza española."

Cuba was ruled, politically, from the time of its discovery until 1812, under the provisions of the celebrated Code of the Indies. The 13th law of the 2d Title, Book the 2d, of that venerable code, reads as follows:

"Porque siendo de una corona los reinos de Castilla y las Indias, las leyes y órden de gobierno de los unos y de los otros deben ser los mas semejantes y conformes que ser puedan."

Therefore, the Cubans were treated during the three first centuries of their existence on the same footing as all other Spaniards, with no difference of any kind; and Cuba followed always, without murmuring, the fate of Spain.

The revolution of 1812 broke out in Spain, and put an end to absolute monarchical rule. A written constitution was granted to Spaniards, and Cuba shared this benefit, and sent her representatives to the Spanish Cortes.

In 1814, on the return of Ferdinand, both Spain and Cuba were again subjected to absolute rule.

In 1820 constitutional government was restored in both the mother country and the island of Cuba.

In 1823, at the bidding of Louis XVIII of France, the absolute power of Ferdinand VII was restored in Spain and Cuba.

In 1834 the *Estatuto Real* placed Cubans again in the possession of the same rights as all other Spaniards. They had again representation in Congress.

In 1837 Cuba held her regular elections, and sent to Spain her representatives; but the Spanish Congress refused to admit them; and enacted an additional article to the constitution of the monarchy, providing that in the future Cuba would be ruled by *special laws*.

One of these laws was the celebrated one giving the governor-general of Cuba *omnimodas facultades*, and the same power over persons and property "*as the governors of besieged places have under the laws of war.*"
This was done in 1837.

From the time of this iniquity to 1868 public feeling was growing more and more hostile to Spain and Spanish rule. The discontent culminated in the outbreak of Yara.

The Cuban war ended as soon as Marshal Martinez Campos agreed to redress the grievances of the Cubans.

This is the text of the capitulation which put an end to the war:

### COMANDANCIA MILITAR DE COLON.

El Ecxmo. Sr. Comandante General de las Villas en telegrama de esta fecha desde Trinidad me dice lo que sigue:

En este momento recibo del E. S. General en Jefe el telegrama siguiente: El Zanjon, Febrero 10 de 1878. He acordado con la Junta central del Camagüey que ha sustituido al Gobierno y Cámara para acordar la Paz, las bases siguientes: "Artículo 1º. Concesion á la Isla de Cuba de las mismas concesiones políticas, orgánicas y administrativas de que disfruta la Isla de Puerto-Rico. 2º. Olvido de lo pasado respecto á los delitos políticos cometidos desde el año 1868 hasta el presente y libertad de los encausados ó que se hallen cumpliendo condena dentro y fuera de la Isla. Indulto general á los desertores del Ejército Español sin distincion de naturalidad, haciendo extensiva esta cláusula á cuantos hubiesen tomado parte directa ó indirectamente en el movimiento revolucionario. 3º. Libertad á los esclavos y colonos asiáticos que se hallan hoy en las filas insurrectas. 4º. Ningun individuo que en virtud de esta capitulacion reconozca y quede bajo la accion del Gobierno Español, podrá ser compelido á prestar ningun servicio de guerra mientras no se establezca la Paz en todo el territorio. 5º. Todo individuo que desée marchar fuera de la Isla queda facultado y se le proporcionará por el Gobierno Español los medios de hacerlo sin tocar en poblacion si así lo descare. Artículo sexto. La capitulacion de cada fuerza se efectuará en despoblado donde con antelacion se depondrán las armas y demás elementos de guerra.—Artículo sétimo. El General en Jefe del ejército Español á fin de facilitar los medios de que puedan avenirse los demás departamentos franqueará todas las vias de mar y tierra de que pueda disponer.—Artículo 8º. Considerar lo pactado con el comité del centro como general y sin restricciones particulares para todos los departamentos de la Isla que acepten estas proposiciones.—Lo manifiesto á V. E. para su conocimiento y las tropas de su mando en la inteligencia que desde luego se suspenderán las operaciones concretándose las tropas á la defensiva y conduccion de comboyes.—En caso de encontrarse enemigos alguna fuerza nuestra, sin romper el fuego les hará conocer estas bases. Así mismo dispondrá V. E. que prácticos acreditados salgan con estas instrucciones á hacerlas conocer á los jefes de las fuerzas contrarias interin lleguen las comisiones de la Junta Central que al efecto salen de esta jurisdiccion.—De órden de S. E.—El General Jefe de E. M. G.—Prendergast."—Lo que tengo la satisfaccion de comunicar á V. S. para conocimiento y á fin de que publicáudose en los periódicos de la localidad y por medio de hojas y otros que el celo de V. S. sugiera, llegue tan fáusto acontecimiento á noticia de todos los habitantes de esa jurisdiccion, sirviéndose remitir ejemplares impresos á los jefes de las columnas en operaciones para su mayor publicidad.—FIGUEROA.

Lo que tengo la satisfaccion de hacer público para general conocimiento de los leales habitantes de esta jurisdiccion.

Colon 11 de Febrero de 1878.

El Coronel Comandante Militar,

JUAN DOMINGO.

*Circulars and decrees of the captain-general of the island of Cuba, for the embargo of property and annihilation of civil rights in 1869.*

SUPERIOR GOVERNORSHIP OF THE PROVINCE OF CUBA.

[Translation.]

It is the duty of all who govern to provide for the security of the territory intrusted to their command. This province being assailed by an insurrection which is beyond appreciation, at whose cry some rich districts of this island are being depopulated and ruined, it becomes indispensable to adopt what measures may be efficient to crush the enemies of our nationality, depriving them principally of all resources which they might rely upon to sustain their aggression.

Therefore, and as it may happen that some sales of property may be executed for illegitimate purposes, in which case such contracts are null, as it is determined by our laws, in the exercise of the extraordinary and discretional powers vested in me by the supreme government of the nation, I resolve to decree the following:

ARTICLE 1. Contracts of sales of real estate or personal property, before being carried into effect, shall after this date be presented for revisal by the government.

ART. 2. To fulfill this order (disposicion), contracts which may be entered into (celebren) in the district of Havana shall be presented at the secretariat of this superior political government, and such as shall be-executed in other jurisdictions of the island at the governors' and lieu tenant-governors'.

ART. 3. The aforesaid presentations, previously to execution, shall be made by the parties interested, when the document is to be of a private nature, and by the notary when it is to become a public deed; in the first of these cases, the original document shall be exhibited, and in the second, the minutes of the deed.

ART. 4. Once revised by the government, the contract cannot be altered or modified in any way without another revisal in advance by the government, under penalty of the correction (reforma) being null.

ART. 5. Sales of produce and other articles of export trade, as well as transfer of stock of anonymous companies, or of special partners (in comandita), become also subject to the prescribed revisal.

ART. 6. When the sales referred to in the preceding article be executed through an authorized broker (corredor de numero), the latter shall present for revisal the contract in the mercantile form it be intended in. If no broker intervenes, the report or presentation shall be made by the contracting parties.

ART. 7. The functionaries of companies anonymous, or with special partners, who, by the respective regulations which bind them, are required to sanction the transfer of shares in the books of the enterprise, will not do so until the government authorize them, for which purpose they will render an account of the transfers intended by parties interested, stating in the communication addressed to the government the name of the contracting parties, their residence, and the manner and value of the shares to be transferred.

ART. 8. In order not to hinder in any manner sales of real estate and personal property and still less, mercantile operations the government shall grant or refuse its approval to the former within four days, and to the sale of produce for export or stock within twenty-four hours from the presentation of the document.

ART. 9. All contracts shall be null of the sale of all kinds of property made without the previous revisal by the government; and private individuals, merchants, brokers, presidents, or directors of anonymous and special partner companies, and notaries public, who shall act in contradiction to what is prescribed in this decree, shall be amenable to the penalties established by the penal code against parties comprised in the chapter 5, title 8, of book 2.

Havana, April 1, 1869.

DOMINGO DULCE.

28

SUPERIOR POLITICAL GOVERNMENT OF THE PROVINCE OF CUBA.

(Circular.)

The mail has brought a printed paper, which is in great circulation, signed by José Morales Lemus, president of the republican central junta of Cuba and Porto Rico.

The reading of the aforesaid document gives rise to important considerations, which I must take notice of, being, as I am, the first and superior authority of this Spanish province, responsible to my country for the integral preservation of its territory.

The fields are defined, and the banner unfurled. Among the enemies of our country, those who run from wood to wood, and start from one hill to another, avoiding to meet our soldiers, are not the most to be feared, because even so acting there is something noble in their cowardice. They struggle in their way, and in most cases they wet the field with their blood. From the commencement they said whither they were going, though it is true they proclaimed the independence of the land of their birth, forgetting that they are and will be Spanish, even against their will, because the language, the religion, the customs, and the life's blood constitute man's true country.

More guilty of the crime of treason are the men who, with feigned humility and base hypocrisy, demanded political rights as the sole remedy to our discord, and responded when granted with providential ingratitude.

From that day their machinations have been the sole and exclusive object of my vigilance. I have from that day followed their steps and even spied their intentions. By adopting preventive measures on a solemn occasion I apprised them that their plans were not unknown to me. Dispossessed (of their hold) and blind, however, they have not kept within the limits of their usual prudence, and in the document alluded to above they are in a hurry to justify the measures already adopted. the resolutions for the immediate application of which your lordship will, or has, received secret instructions; and the system of unflinching rigor which I have determined to follow, and which is more necessary at present when the armed rebellion is agonizing, than at the time when in the east and west, and in the central department it showed itself ostentatious and boasted of its strength.

The aforesaid document, which, were its suggestions obeyed, would furnish its authors with a golden mine to minister to their vices and individual profit, is intended to frighten the timid, to flatter and encourage the avaricious, and to threaten men loyal to Spanish tradition, who will never be perfidious traitors.

As your lordship will understand, neither respect to doctrines, nor the worship of principles, especially now that the political and administrative legitimacy of our country is a mystery of the future, shall deter me in traversing the path, however rugged, which the tranquillity of the families and the saving of property advises me.

The armed insurrection being controlled and conquered, it follows forcibly, as required by the convenience of all, in accordance with equity and public sentiment, that the severe execution of certain laws shall drain the source whence the hidden instigators of the unnatural (fratricidal) strife draw resources.

I therefore enjoin on you to have prudent watchfulness; do not allow

29

a noisy overflow of patriotism to compromise the execution of the orders
your lordship may have received or shall receive in the future.

Any omission or oversight, however trifling, would impose on me the
painful duty of punishing with all the severity of the law.

God preserve your lordship many years.

Havana, 15th April, 1869.

DOMINGO DULCE.

To the governor ———.

[Official.]

(*From the Diaro de la Marina of 21st April,* 1869.)

SUPERIOR POLITICAL GOVERNMENT OF THE PROVINCE OF CUBA.

(Circular.)

By the Gazette of 15th instant you will have been informed of two
circulars issued by me : the first on the occasion of receiving by mail
and circulating of a paper signed José Morales Lemus, president of the
central republican junta of Cuba and Porto Rico, and the second ordering the immediate embargo of the estates and other properties that said
Morales Lemus and other individuals possess or may have possessed on
this island.

You will have likewise become acquainted with my decree of 1st instant, published in the Gazette of the 16th, as a preventive measure to
impede sales of property made with illegitimate ends ; and lastly, in
the Gazette of the 18th, an administrative committee has been appointed
to administer the property embargoed by the decree of 1st instant.
These resolutions, well considered and justified by the damages caused
by the insurgents, appertain to a system which is indispensable to follow in order to put an end to the insurrection at once. To obtain this
object, and exercising the extraordinary and discretional powers with
which I am invested by the supreme government of the nation, I have
determined the following :

ARTICLE 1. All persons to whom it may be proved that they have
taken part in the insurrection, in or out of the island either armed or
aiding the same with arms. ammunitions, money or provisions, are
hereby declared to be comprised in the circular of 15th inst., relative
to José Morales Lemus and others.

ART. 2. The persons who within the proper time claimed the benefit
of the amnesty and pardon decreed, and who in their subsequent conduct have proved their adhesion to the government, are excepted from
the above resolution.

ART. 3. The persons comprised in Article 1st are hereby deprived of
the *political and civil rights* which they enjoyed through our laws, the
action of this resolution being carried back to the 10th of October, when
the insurrection of Yara commenced, or back to the date in which it
may be ascertained that they took part in the preparations for the insurrection.

ART. 4. The contracts agreed to by said individuals, from the dates
above mentioned, shall be presented to the revisal of the government
within three days after the publication of this circular.

ART. 5. The governors and lieutenant-governors will immediately
remit said contracts, with their report, to the president of the administrative council, where, in view of the antecedents, the proper resolutions will be decided upon.

ART. 6. Said authorities shall at once proceed by themselves, or through their delegates, to institute a government investigation to prove the crime of the parties comprised in this resolution, giving an account to the president of the administrative council of the commencement of said investigation.

ART. 7. As the guilt of the delinquents shall become established, the embargo of their properties, actions, and rights shall be acted upon, and the governors of the other districts where they may also have property shall be informed, so that those shall be also embargoed.

ART. 8. Each governmental investigating process shall refer to one individual alone, and as it shall be brought to conclusion with the deposit of the property embargoed, the council of administration shall be informed in conformity with the Art. 7th of the decree creating said council.

ART. 9. The governors and lieutenant-governors, who in their jurisdiction should embargo property of individuals who had been or are residents in another jurisdiction, will remit to the president of the administrative council the items referred to in the article quoted in the preceding, and will communicate to the governor from whence the embargo proceeds a statement of the property embargoed, which shall be annexed to the government proceeding.

ART. 10. When the opportunity arrive from the state of the procedure to embargo property, an order shall be issued stating the grounds, and shall be carried into effect by the same lieutenant-governor, or the delegate appointed by him, assisted by the notary or secretary (escribano), and either two or three witnesses, who should be near relatives of the delinquent, or, if there be none such, his near neighbors. In the absence of a notary, two witnesses shall be employed, according to law.

ART. 11. In the act of the embargo an exact inventory of the property taken, reporting the same in detail, discriminating furniture, real estate, rights, and shares or actions, circumstances being set forth to establish their indentity and avoid all mistakes.

ART. 12. The property embargoed shall be deposited in a resident lego (not a lawyer), llano (not privileged from rank or class), and abonado (enjoying guaranty for the object), selected by the governor or lieutenant-governor, who shall inform the president of the administrative council of said appointment, and give the depositary a certified copy of the embargo, and of his appointment.

ART. 13. It is left to the judgment of the governor, or lieutenant-governor, as the case may be, to deliver all the property to a single depositary, or to distribute it among several ; said authorities bearing in mind that the best possible means should be adopted that the property may not be injured in its nature or productiveness ; for which motive, if there should be some creditor (refaccionista) (one who provides the necessary to sustain and bring about the profits of an enterprise), they will endeavor to have the same appointed as depositary (receiver), provided said party deserve the full confidence of the authority.

ART. 14. The depositaries shall take charge of the property in accordance with the inventory, giving receipt before the lieutenant-governor or his delegate, witnesses, and the attesting notary, and said depositaries binding themselves with their persons and property to have said property safely guarded as a judicial deposit, subject to the order of the president of the administrative council.

ART. 15. The depositaries shall preserve and administer the property with all care and diligence, being responsible even for slight faults ;

they shall not be authorized to sell it for no reason or pretext excepting when the governor or lieutenant-governor should order it in consequence of a resolution of the administrative council ; they shall neither be authorized to transfer the deposit to another party, unless for a just cause it should be ordered by the first authority in the district, in which case the newly-appointed depositary shall take charge of the property in accordance with the preceding article, all of which shall be made known to the president of the administrative council.

ART. 16. The depositaries (receivers) shall keep a faithful, exact account, with vouchers, of all expenses originated, and of the products yielded by the property, which account, together with the net profits, they will present monthly to the governor or lieutenant-governor.

ART. 17. As soon as the depositary (receiver) shall have sent the net result, the first authority shall order their ingress in the treasury department, with the character of a deposit, subject to the order of the president of the administrative council, to whom the formal receipts shall be sent, a certified copy of which shall be left in the proceedings.

ART. 18. The accounts, with their vouchers, shall also be sent to the president of the administrative council, that he may do the needful until their approval, and a copy of the decree of approval shall be sent to the lieutenant-governor, to have it annexed to the procedure.

ART. 19. When the property embargoed should be found to be *haciendas* (estates), cattle, or other requiring culture or collection, the depositary shall be authorized to select and appoint, on his responsibility, the manager or clerks strictly needed.

ART. 20. No one who is not by law dispensed from exercising municipal duties can exempt himself from serving the functions of depositary. In proportion to the importance and quality of the property embargoed, and also to the labor required of the depositary, the governor or lieutenant-governor shall report to the president of the administrative council respecting the compensation that the former should receive, which should always consist in a percentage on the sums collected and paid by him, with the understanding that it shall not exceed five per cent. for each of said objects, the amount of profits returned referred to in article 16 being exempted from said charge.

ART. 21. The governors and lieutenant-governors shall be answerable in conformity to the laws for the improper selection by them made of depositaries, and, therefore, for the errors committed by the latter, especially if through their fault the embargoed property should perish.

ART. 22. The property embargoed shall be answerable in the first place for the expenses incurred for its preservation and management, those to be preferred consisting in current and arrear taxes, and for next debts contracted by the owner of the embargoed property, previously to the dates referred to in article 3d.

ART. 23. If the creditor should be one of the individuals referred to in this circular, the payment of the accredited claims shall be made into the hands of the depositary of the property embargoed of said creditor. If the latter should not be of that class he should be made to prove his claims before the governor and lieutenant-governor, who shall report to the president of the administrative council, who, when the case shall justify it, shall order the payment. The debts contracted after the dates referred to article 3d will be made subject to the resolution in articles 4 and 5.

ART. 24. When all or a portion of the property sequestrated or embargoed shall be found subject to an association of creditors before a court, or to a judicial procedure in a failure, the common attorney representing creditors (*sindico*) may be appointed depositary, but if said *sindicos* or attorneys should have been appointed by the court where the case belongs to, then they are of necessity to be appointed depositaries of the embargo under the obligation of fulfilling the enactments of this circular relative to said depositaries.

The attorneys (*sindicos*) remunerated by said association of creditors (*concurso*) will not receive the remuneration to which article 20 refers.

ART. 25. Once the sentence for the order of payments shall have been given in the court where the creditors are represented, as soon as it shall be ready for execution, a copy of it shall be annexed to the government procedure for the needful objects, and the governor or lieutenant-governor shall send a copy to the president of the administrative council.

ART. 26. In cases where the property embargoed in consequence of the government precedure should have been embargoed in advance judicially by order of a court, the new embargo shall be made known to the judge who ordered the first. In this case the depositary already named shall be appointed anew, and also receive the deposit, going over the counting and making another inventory of the property; but with no assignation of stipend, unless he should have been entitled to it by the first appointment committed to him.

ART. 27. If the first embargo should have been established at the request of some one of those to whom this circular refers, when the criminality of said individual shall have been proven in the governmental proceeding, the governor or lieutenant-governor shall communicate the fact to the respective judge, who, after having the law expenses apprized, shall suspend the course of the proceedings, sending them to the government authority that it may order the payment of said expenses, and whatever else should be required, according to article 23d.

ART. 28. When the first embargo is made at the request of a party not comprised in this circular, the respective judges shall dictate the sentence according to law in the shortest possible term, sending copy of it to the governor or lieutenant-governor for the objects that may be required.

ART. 29. If any person not comprised in this circular should claim as his, all or a part of the property embargoed, the embargo shall not be raised until his right shall have been proved, and until the administrative council shall have issued its decision, and to said council report shall be made of the case, with the proceedings.

ART. 30. The governor, or lieutenant-governor, who, in his jurisdiction should embargo property of individuals who were, or are residents of another jurisdiction, will initiate the proceedings with the communication he may receive for the embargo, executing the same immediately, in conformity to the terms of this circular.

Said proceedings once ended, the governor or lieutenant-governor shall comply with what is required in article 9th, keeping said proceedings in the government office for subsequent ends.

ART. 31. When the order for the embargo, referred to in article 10th shall be given, parties possessing money, goods, or values of any kind, belonging to the individual concerned in the proceedings, shall be summoned through the newspapers or public bulletins, to report to the government authority, and be made responsible for any concealment or act intended to evade the said resolutions, it being forbidden expressly to buy, sell, pay, transfer, give or do aught which may affect, or which refers to the ownership of the goods embargoed, with the understanding that infractors shall be attained in what is determined regarding offenses involving treason in the decree of this superior government, dated 13th of February last, and they shall be consequently subjected to a council of war.

God preserve you many years.

Habana, 20th of April, 1869.

DOMINGO DULCE.

Addressed to all governors or lieutenant-governors.

___

### SUPERIOR GOVERNORSHIP OF THE PROVINCE OF CUBA.

In the exercise of the extraordinary and discretional powers invested in me by the supreme government of the nation, and with a view to the necessity and urgency of executing with all proper legality, solemnity, and publicity the acts resulting from the embargo of property of all kind appertaining to the sixteen individuals referred to in the communication addressed to the political governor of this district, on the 1st instant, and of all who may be in the same case, I come to the resolution to decree the following:

1. A board is hereby established to administer property belonging to the sixteen individuals referred to in my decree of 1st instant, which were ordered to be embargoed on the same date.

2. Said administrative council is composed of the political governor of Havana, as president; of three members from the corporation of this capital; three from the class of proprietors and planters; three from the class of merchants; one superior officer, from the financial department; a secretary, who shall be the secretary of the political governorship, and of such employés as shall be proposed to me by the president of the aforesaid council.

3. The functions of president, members, and secretary of the council shall receive no compensation.

4. All funds collected in consequence of the embargoes shall be deposited in the general treasury, whence receipts shall be issued for the security of the president of the administrative council—the funds being subject to his order.

5. The president of said board will have authority to decide all matters and points offering doubt in the interpretation of my decree of 1st instant, and those of a judicial or legal nature calling for decisions from the established courts shall only be brought to me for resolution.

6. The appointment and removal of individuals to fill the bureaus of the administrative council shall be determined by said president. The salaries of said functionaries and the cost of articles required shall be defrayed from the funds collected.

7. The lieutenant-governor of this province shall remit to the president of the administrative council all items they may acquire in their respective districts relating to property embargoed, or to such as may be hereafter embargoed; they shall deliver said property to the same council, together with the inventories, deeds, and other public documents which they may acquire or consider necessary; and they shall execute such orders referring said matters as they may receive from said president.

8. The president of the aforesaid board shall propose to my authority whatever change in the organization of the same, or in the persons composing it, he may consider expedient to make.

Havana, April 17th, 1869.

DOMINGO DULCE.

3 SP

34

SUPERIOR GOVERNORSHIP OF THE PROVINCE OF CUBA.

In conformity with the requirements of my decree of this date, and exercising the extraordinary powers invested in me by the supreme government of the nation, I have resolved to appoint president of the council to administer property ordered to be embargoed belonging to sixteen individuals, referred to in my order of 1st instant, and of as many more as may be in the same circumstances, Don Dionisio Lopez Roberts, political governor of Havana, and members (of the board) Don Juan Atilano Colomé, Don Mamerto Pulido, and Count Posor-Dulces, from the corporation of this capital; Don José Cabargo, Don Juan Poey and Don Joaquin Pedroso, as proprietors and planters; Don Fernando Illas, Don Bonifacio Jimenez and Don Segundo Rigal, merchants; Don Agustus Genou, as chief of the central section of taxes and statistics, and Secretary Don Juan Zaragosa, who is secretary of the political governorship of Havana.

Havana April 17, 1869.

DOMINGO DULCE.

_____

NOTE No. 7.

OFFICE OF THE CAPTAIN-GENERAL OF THE EVER FAITHFUL ISLAND OF CUBA—ETAT MAJEUR.—BUREAU NO. 7.

The Governor-General wrote to me on the 27th ultimo, what follows: "It is a notorious fact that the Cuban refugees in New York have appointed a so-called republican government of Cuba, and an auxiliary junta to make war against Spain, and that they support various periodicals for the same object. The names of the members of the revolutionary government are published in said paper, together with their revolutions and the false statement of frequent victories over our troops, and _notwithstanding this, no charge of high treason against those persons_, who are well known to all, has yet been made. _Public order raises its voice against such an omission_, which was, no doubt, dictated by the hope, a frustrated one, that they would desist from their plans, which at the beginning could be considered as a manifestation of ideas more or less radical, in favor of a reformation in the government of the island. I communicate this to you, in order that you may appoint an officer possessing all special requirement, who will proceed to the institution of criminal proceedings against the persons compromised as leaders in the so-called government, and the 'Junta auxiliar,' citing them and fixing such terms as to allow them to answer the charges brought against them. For that purpose, I send herewith to your excellency two copies of the periodical La Revolucion, of June 26 and August 11, giving some names; the communication of the others shall follow as they are obtained."

And I transmit this to you in order that you may proceed in the capacity of judge-advocate to the institution of said proceedings. For that purpose I inclose the two mentioned copies of the periodical La Revolucion. Furthermore, you will nominate at once the officer of the garrison, being presently in this place, whom you may deem fit to serve in this case as your secretary.

May God preserve you many years.

Havana, September the 2nd, 1869.

CABALLERO.

To Don FRANCISCO MONTAOS, _a colonel of cavalry._

NOTE No. 8.

CAPTAIN-GENERALSHIP OF THE ISLAND OF CUBA, STAFF.

*The drumhead court-martial*, sitting at this place on this day, with the object of examining and judging into the process instituted against the civilian, José Valdez Nodarse, for having uttered seditious words, has condemned him to six years' hard labor in the chain gang; and his excellency in conformity with the opinion of the auditor has been pleased to approve said sentence, but recognizing, as the auditor does, too great lenity in the sentence, because it is not in accord with the regulations, codes, and existing laws, he has ordered *that the president and members of the military court may be sent to a castle to suffer the penalty of two months' imprisonment in the same.*
Published by order of his excellency.
Havana, December 24, 1869.

CARLO NAVARRO,
*Brigadier-General, Commanding the Staff.*
Gaceta de la Habana, number of December 25, 1869.

NOTE No. 9.

GOBIERNO SUPERIOR POLÍTICO DE LA PROVINCIA DE CUBA.

EXCMO. SR. Antes dé que V. E. le dispensára la houra de nombrarle Secretario de este Gobierno Superior Político, dedicóse el que suscribe al estudio de la grave trascendental cuestion del embargo de los bienes de los infidentes ó sospechosos de infidencia y la debatió en la prensa de esta ciudad tomando por criterio el mismo que le parecia tener el Gobierno Supremo respecto de aquellos contra quienes por las pruebas recogidas resultaban méritos suficientes para ser juzgados y condenados por los Tribunales y de este Gobierno Superior Político en cuanto á aquellos contra quienes solo aparecian sospechas, presunciones ó indicios, y seguro de que en sus soluciones no se apartaba de la Ley, ha aplicado despues de ser Secretario de V. E. las mismas doctrinas á los casos prácticos que se han sometido á su informe teniendo la buena suerte de que el Excmo. Consejo de Administracion aquí y luego el Gobierno Supremo las haya aprobado con honrosas frases.
Pero á pesar de esto ha notado que las resoluciones dictadas por V. E., y lo que la sana razon y el interés de matar en su raiz el mal de la rebelion aconsejan, no se obtienen los resultados que son de desear, ya porque no se han definido bien la esfera en que han de girar el Consejo administrativo de bienes y sus relaciones con el Gobierno Superior Político, ya porque las disposiciones dictadas para los casos de reclamacion de algunos acreedores lejítimos contra esos bienes, no se han comprendido bien, ya por otras razones que por ser muy sabidas de V. E., se escusa el que suscribe de repetirlas ahora. Y como este mal ha andado acompañado de conflictos desagradables entre dicho Consejo y la Secretaría de V. E., el que suscribe se ha sentido obligado á poner el dedo en la llaga, profundizando más sus estudios y proponiendo, como fruto de ellos, un radical remedio en la presente mocion.
Afortunadamente no le ha sido difícil alcanzar el ver la raiz del mal. Ha consistido y consiste éste en que habiendo dispuesto el Gobierno Supremo que se suprima el Consejo administrativo de bienes creándose

en su lugar uno meramente consultivo, y llenando V. E. los vacíos de esa disposicion por el desconocimiento en el Ministerio de Ultramar de todos los datos y noticias necesarias, no se haya dado, por una parte, entero cumplimiento á ella y su instruccion adjunta, ni por otra se haya elevado al Gobierno Supremo una exposicion clara de las varias cuestiones que nacen de los embargos y de la resolucion mas conveniente á los fines que al hacerlos se han tenido presentes.

Tambien ha reconocido otro orígen el mal, cual es que, al ménos al parecer, se ha cuidado mas de reservar la integridad de las fincas embargadas, rigiéndose por el erróneo celo de que resulte mas pura por ese medio la administracion de ellas, que de tener presente que los embargos llevan por primordial objeto evitar recursos á la rebelion, castigar á los rebeldes, y por ámbos medios salvar la integridad del territorio; cuyo criterio ha producido necesariamente la consecuencia dolorosa de salir castigados los acreedores españoles por la razon sencilla de no ser pagados á tiempo sus créditos con la enagenacion de los bienes á ellos afectos, por no vender éstos, V. E. dictó una disposicion encaminada á enderezar este entuerto; pero desgraciadamente no ha sido bien cumplida.

Y á que sean cumplidas esa como las demás se dirige, Excmo. Sr., esta mocion, ya que V. E. puede hacerlo con que sea una verdad de hecho el decreto de 25 de marzo de este año, toda vez que en su preámbulo se espone que confía el Gobierno en que donde no alcancen las disposiciones de la instruccion que le acompaña, el celo de la Autoridad Superior y económica de esta Isla, con su exquisita vigilancia suplirá lo necesario para conseguir el fin que el Gobierno se propone.

Por de pronto, Excmo. Sr., el arrendamiento de las fincas embargadas es imposible tal como se previene en esas disposiciones lo que comprenderá V. E. al leer en ellas que se hagan los arrendamientos por un año pagándose en cuanto á las rústicas el 25 p. $\frac{3}{2}$ al tiempo de otorgarse la escritura y el 75 p.$\frac{3}{2}$ restante al empezarse la molienda ; porque no habria quien hiciera postura bajo estas condiciones, que no guardan armonía con la naturaleza de los ingenios y grandes haciendas ganaderas de este pais, y á más esa conservacion de lo embargado en su cabal integridad, hace imposible el pago de los acreedores y la realizacion de las incautaciones prevenidas en las sentencias dictadas en Consejo de Guerra para hacer efectiva la responsabilidad civil que como pena accesoria se dicta juntamente con la corporal á fin de que ambas sean impuestas.

La conservacion en administracion tansolo de los bienes embargados precautoriamente en virtud del decreto de 20 de abril de 1869, siendo libres, es decir, no teniendo sobre sí gravámen, ni reclamacion, y la venta de lo mandado incautar es lo que únicamente responde á todos los derechos, Excmo. Sr., porque está dentro de la Ley y la observancia de esta es la suprema necesidad de la vida de las sociedades, pues el cumplimiento de la Ley, justificando esta venta, no solo hace justo al Gobierno, sino que le honra como recto Juzgador.

Espuesta estas consideraciones, pasa el que suscribe á detallar las varias cuestiones que se suscitan con motivo de esos embargos y á proponer la resolucion que corresponde en cada caso.

En el decreto en cuestion se habla en general de embargos de bienes, y no debe ser así, sino que debe establecerse una distincion, que segun la clase del embargo y la calidad de lo embargado ha de producir consecuencias diversas. El decreto de 20 de abril se propuso tan solo privar á los sospechosos de infidencia de los medios de prestar auxilio á la insurreccion, y ha solido hacerse, y se hacen los embargos á que se refiere, por datos de presuncion ó indicios, sin aguardar á tener prueba completa, de modo que, como muchas veces se desvanecen estos ó el interesado hace prueba en contrario, esos embargos, sujetos á alzamientos, tienen tan solo el carácter de preventivos ó pracautorios, y así lo ha reconocido el Ministerio de Ultramar al sancionar con aplauso las reglas aquí dictadas para resolver los casos de desembargo con arreglo á una jurisprudencia cierta y constante. Por otra parte, para que se acomodaran los consejos de guerra al derecho penal que invocan para penar los casos de infidencia á ellos sujetos, que es el derecho comun, toda vez que el delito no es especial, ó snjeto al Código militar y la lógica exgía que quien se rija por una ley la tenga toda presente aplicando de ella, no una parte, cual es la pena corporal, sino tambien las accesorias, de las que una es la indemnizacion de daños y perjuicios ocasionados por el delito, se han dictado alguuas disposiciones por V. E. para que al iniciarse una causa de infidencia, dicten los fiscales instructores de los sumarios auto de embargo en cuanto aparezcan datos de culpabilidad contra determinada persona, y porque tambien en todas las sentencias condenatorias se provea la incautacion de dichos bienes á fin de que llenen la responsabilidad accesoria, con lo cual queda ya determinado que estos embargos son diferentes en su origen y en su objeto de los primeros.

Tambieu cabe notable diferencia en la calidad de los bienes embargados: unos son libres, es decir, no tienen sobre sí carga alguna, miéntras que otros, ya por gravámen hipotecario ó censario, ya por estar sujetos á un juic'o pendiente en los Tribunales ordinarios, no pueden responder en su totalidad, ni al objeto de los embargos precautorios, ni al fin de su incautacion por el Estado en cumplimiento de una sentencia ejecutoria. Ni aquellos embargos, ni estas incautaciones pueden ser en daño de tercero, y claro es que teniendo anterior y legalmente una responsabilidad que limita la totalidad de su valor, el Estado debe dejar libre esta, concretándose al embargo ó incautacion del *todo*, *ménos* lo que importa esa responsabilidad.

Pero aun hay más. Los bienes incautados en virtud de sentencia ejecutoria para las indemnizaciones de los daños causados por el delito, tampoco son de la misma clase, pues unos lo han sido en causa de reo presente, y otros en proceso de reo ausente, que ha sido juzgado por lo mismo en rebeldía, y la ley vigente es diferente en cada uno de los casos. Juzgado un reo presente y condenado á la pena accesoria de la indemnizacion, sus bienes deben ser incautados por el Estado y vendidos inmediatamente en pública subasta, ingresando su importe en arcas reales con ese destino. Sentenciado y condenado en rebeldía un reo, sus bienes deben ser incautados por la Hacienda, administrados por la Administracion central de propiedades del Estado, con informe del Consejo consultivo que se forme, y al año de la fecha de la sentencia vendidos en remate como lo previene la ley vigente 1. a, título 37, libro 12, de la Novísima recopilacion que dice: "y pasado el dicho año no se habiendo dentro del presentado ni prendido, el tal acusado, se ejecute luego la sentencia en las penas de dineros ó de bienes, así en las que se aplicaren á la nuestra cámara ó fisco como en las que se aplicaren á la parte, y no pueda en cuanto á ellas ser oido aunque pasado el dicho año se presente á la cárcel; pero presentándose pasado el año, ó seyendo preso, sea oido en cuanto á las penas corporales solamente y no sobre las de dinero ó bienes como dicho es."

Ya ve V. E. que si dificultades y conflictos ofrece hoy la constitucion anómala del Consejo administrativo de bienes embargados, es por que no se observa la ley: esta pues debe cumplirse en todas sus partes: aquí viene de molde el principio "dura lex, sed lex." El derecho de la justicia inexorable está interesado en que los bienes embargados sean destinados á lo que se debe, ya como castigo del culpable, ya al pago de acreedores legítimos, que con anterioridad al embargo tienen derechos imprescindibles que no deben ser, que no pueden ser burlados sin cometerse una tremenda injusticia, porque si esos acreedores son buenos españoles, resulta que en vez de castigar al malo, se daña al leal, y si son extranjeros, se dá ocasion á que acudan á su Gobierno, y haciendo caso de diplomacia, gestionen cuantiosas reclamaciones por indemnizacion.

Finalmente; falta que fijar la jurisprudencia sobre otro punto.—V. E. es la única autoridad que decreta y puede decretar esos embargos precautorios en virtud del decreto de 20 de abril de 1869, por consiguiente V. E. es el único tambien que puede fijar hasta donde alcanza ese embargo. Algunas veces hecho el embargo en unos bienes acuden los acreedores al Consejo; pero este demora la calificacion meses y meses, y entónces apelan aquellos ante V. E.: V. E. los oye y con informe del Consejo, resuelve. Esta resolucion debe ser cumplida por el Consejo sin excusa. Otras veces esos acreedores vienen pidiendo á V. E. la declaratoria de un derecho sobre esos bienes, y V. E. es tambien la única autoridad competente para concederlo ó negarlo: la resolucion de V. E. no puede tener réplica por el Consejo y siempre es V. E. autoridad de apelacion de las disposiciones que tome el Consejo, si alguna vez, excediéndose de sus facultades, de consultivo se convierte en resolutivo. Esta doctrina es aplicable tambien a la Intendencia, si V. E. aceptando este informe, resuelve de conformidad con él.

Sentada esta doctrina, que no tiene réplica en la esfera de la justicia, y está conforme con las disposiciones hasta ahora dictadas, la resolucion procedente, es muy obvia, la supresion del actual Consejo administrativo de bienes embargados y la creacion del consultivo, á fin de dar á esos bienes el destino que deben tener segun los principios expuestos: de cuyo exacto cumplimiento debe encargarse la Intendencia, y esto es lo que el que sucribe propone á V. E., rogandole lo sancione con su superior criterio y mandato.

Habana 31 de julio de 1871.

RAMON MARÍA DE ARAÍSTEGUI.

RESOLUCION.

Visto el decreto de 25 marzo de 1871, y la instruccion que le acompaña, y las demás disposiciones vigentes, y de conformidad con la Secretaria; Vengo en resolver que quede desde luego suprimido el actual Consejo administrativo de bienes embargados, dando gracias á los señores que lo componen por los servicios prestados, y que se proceda á la creacion del Cuerpo consultivo de la Administracion central de Propiedades del Estado que deberá establecerse inmediatamente para los fines á que deben ser destinados los bienes embargados, segun su clase y responsabilidades, al tenor de las disposiciones vigentes, proponiéndome el Intendente de Hacienda las personas competentes para su formacion: declaro tambien que me reservo, con la facultad de decretar embargos precautorios, al tenor de lo dispuesto en el decreto de 20 de abril de 1869, la de fijar hasta cuanto ha de subir ese embargo, la de desembargar totalmente, y la de resolver sin ulterior recurso las reclamaciones que en queja, apelacion ó de otro modo establezcan los interesados en los bienes embargados contra lo que el Consejo y la Intendencia determinen sobre ellos, salvo todo lo que el Gobierno Supremo disponga.—Comuníquese esta disposicion á la Intendencia para su inmediato cumplimiento.

VALMASEDA.

39

## Note No. 10.

*Decree of King Amadeo.*

### EXPOSICION.

Señor: Por el decreto que V. M. se ha servido expedir con fecha 9 de los corrientes, se destina entre otros arbitrios, á la amortizacion de billetes del Banco Español de la Habana, emitidos por cuenta del Tesoro, el producto de los bienes embargados en Cuba á los insurrectos é infidentes en virtud de providencia de los tribunales. Esta medida, sin embargo, será incompleta si no se adoptase otra con respecto á los bienes embargados por providencia gubernativa.

Hay, en efecto, bienes de esta última situacion, y el gobierno, por más que el hecho sea inevitable consecuencia de la insurreccion cubana, no producido por él é independiente de su voluntad, tiene la obligacion de someter sus consecuencias á reglas en lo posible fijas y ordenadas. El embargo de bienes á los insurrectos de Cuba es á la vez un medio de asegurar el castigo de los delincuentes, y un acto de legitima defensa que la nacion ejecuta para mantener su integridad; más por lo mismo conviene que conserve ambos caractéres, y que no haya razon para calificarle de arbitrario y caprichoso. Con el fin de conseguirlo, parece necesario que se proceda á una revision de todos los espedientes de embargo gubernativo, y que mediante ella se haga la debida distincion entre los casos.

Si los hay tales que en ellos existan pruebas suficientes de delincuencia contra los dueños de los bienes, deben ser sometidos al conocimiento dé los tribunales; y si estos decretan la continuacion del embargo, el propósito queda conseguido con plena seguridad, con la seguridad más grande de cuantas reconocen las leyes. Cuando las pruebas de criminalidad no sean bastantes, y haya sin embargo fundadas presunciones, el propósito se consigue rodeando á la accion gubernativa de garantias de imparcialidad y de acierto, disponiendo que sus actos no sean definitivos, y evitando que las consecuencias de lo que se ejecute sean irreparables. Así sucederá si el alzamiento ó confirmacion de los embargos son decretados por la autoridad politica de Cuba, despues de oir el parecer de una tan respetable corporacion como la Junta de la deuda mandada crear por el arriba citado decreto.

Con esta medida se pondrá órden y concierto con el hecho mismo de los embargos. Pero necesitándose además atender á las consecuencias del hecho, hay que dictar algunas otras medidas:

Es, por ejemplo, indispensable dar alguna regla para apreciar equitativa y justamente la situacion en que queden los productos de los bienes embargados. Los productos deben entrar como una especie de depósito en las arcas del Tesoro, pero deben salir de ellas, sea para aplicarlos á la amortizacion de billetes cuando el embargo se confirme por los tribunales, sea para su devolúcion á los dueños de los bienes cuando el embargo se levante por los tribunales ó por la misma autoridad gubernativa.

De igual modo debe ser reglamentada y ordenada la administracion y custodia de los bienes gubernativamente embargados. Para ello nada mejor que estender á estos bienes lo ya establecido respecto de los embargados judicialmente; esto es, encargar de la administracion y custodia á la Junta de la deuda.

El conjunto de estas medidas es, en opinion del ministro que suscribe, suficiente para dar á la accion administrativa la fijeza y rectitud de que siempre debe ir resuelta, y que imperiosamente exije la opinion de tan importante y delicado asunto.

Para ello tiené la honra, de acuredo con el Consejo de Ministros, de proponer á la aprobacion de V. M. el adjunto proyecto de decreto.

Madrid 6 de agosto de 1872.

El ministro de Ultramar.

EDUARDO GASSET Y ARTIME.

DECRETO.

En vista de las razones que me ha expuesto el ministro de Ultramar, y de acuerdo con el Consejo de Ministros, vengo en decretar lo siguiente:

ARTÍCULO 1°. Los bienes que están ó en adelante sean embargados por providencia gubernativa á los insurrectos é infidentes en la isla de Cuba, serán administrados por la Junta de la Deuda del Tesoro, creada por decreto de 9 de este mes.

ART. 2°. La administracion de estos bienes será llevada por la Junta con sujecion á las bases prescritas en el art. 15 del mismo decreto para la de los bienes embargados por providencia de los tribunales.

ART. 3°. Los bienes gubernativamente embargados se clasificarán en dos categorías.

La primera comprenderá los de personas que estén en la insurreccion ó de cuya complicidad con los insurrectos haya pruebas bastantes.

La segunda comprenderá los de personas de cuya complicidad con los insurrectos no haya pruebas bastantes, aunque haya presunciones fundadas.

La clasificacion será hecha por la Junta y aprobada por el Gobernador Superior civil, con audiencia de los interesados si la pidieren.

ART. 4°. Hecha la clasificacion de los bienes, el Gobernador Superior civil pasará á los tribunales correspondientes los datos relativos á los dueños de los bienes comprendidos en la primera categoría.

Si los tribunales confirmaran el embargo, seguirán los bienes administrados por la Junta. Si le alzaran, se devolverán los bienes á sus dueños.

ART. 5°. Respecto de los bienes comprendidos en la segunda categoría, el Gobernador Superior civil dispondrá que la Junta revise los expedientes; y oido su parecer, así como las reclamaciones de los interesados, decretará la continuacion ó alzamiento de los embargos.

ART. 6°. Cuando decrete la continuacion, el Gobernador Superior civil dispondrá que sigan abiertos los expedientes, á fin de llevar á ellos cuantos datos se adquieran sobre la inocencia de los dueños ó su complicidad con la insurreccion.

La misma autoridad, con audiencia de la Junta, y examinadas las reclamaciones que hubieren hecho los interesados, decidirá que pasen á la primera categoría los bienes de que trata este artículo, y remitirá los expedientes á los tribunales siempre que se hayan adquirido pruebas suficientes de la criminalidad de los dueños.

ART. 7°. Los expedientes gubernativos sobre desembargos que estén pendientes de resolucion se unirán á los de embargo de los bienes respectivos, y se someterán á la clasificacion y revision de que hablan los artículos 3° y 5°.

Del mismo modo se unirán, á fin de ser tramitadas con ellos, á los expedientes de embargo las solicitudes de desembargo que se hagan en lo sucesivo.

ART. 8°. Los embargos que en adelante se decreten, serán inmediatamente pasados á los tribunales, si el Gobernador Superior civil, oyendo á la Junta, estimare que hay pruebas bastantes respecto de la criminalidad de los dueños de los bienes.

Cuando no sean pasados á los tribunales, se observará en cuanto á ellos lo prevenido en el art. 5º.

ART. 9º. El Gobernador Superior civil tomará las medidas convenientes par que la Junta se encargue, en cuante esté instalada, de la administracion de los bienes embargados por providencia gubernativa.

ART. 10º. La Junta entregará mensualmente en las arcas del tesoro los productos que recaude de estos bienes.

ART. 11º. Los productos de los bienes correspondientes á la primera categoría, cuyo embargo sea confirmado por los tribunales, serán aplicados á la amortizacion de los billetes, con arreglo al decreto de 9 de este mes; y para ello entrarán de nuevo en poder de la Junta, si esta los hubiere entregado al Tesoro.

ART. 12º. Los demas productos serán devueltos á los dueños de los bienes ó á sus herederos en los siguientes casos:

Los de bienes de la primera categoría, cuando los tribunales llamados á conocer con arreglo á los artículos 4º, 6º y 8º decreten el alzamiento del embargo por falta de mérito para proceder contra los dueños.

Los de bienes de la segunda categoría, cuando el gobernador superior civil disponga el alzamiento del embargo conforme al artº 5º.

ART. 13º. La Junta redactará una instruccion para llevar á efecto lo prevenido en este decreto, y la someterá á la aprobacion del gobernador superior civil. Si este la aprueba, se pondrá en vigor desde luego, y sin perjuicio de la resolucion que sobre ella se adopte por el ministerio de ultramar, al que será remitida para su definitiva aprobacion.

ART. 14º. Quedan derogadas todas las disposiciones vigentes sobre bienes embargados en Cuba por providencia gubernativa, en cuanto se opongan á las prescripciones de este decreto.

Dado en palacio á treinta y uno de agosto de 1872.

AMADEO.

El ministro de ultramar.

EDUARDO GASSET Y ARTIME.

## NOTE No. 11.

Mr. Hall, United States consul-general at Havana, in his report of June 20, 1877, said: "The practice of the junta of embargoed property appears to have been, in this case as well as in others, to collect all the incomes, to sell all the products, and to pay none of the liabilities of the estate."

## NOTE No. 12.

*Decree of July 12, 1873, revoking embargoes in Cuba.*

### PREAMBLE.

Animated by the principles of strict legality, which form the unchangeable foundation of democratic teachings, and desirous of realizing, in all that pertains to his department, the amplest attainable right, the undersigned minister has endeavored with zealous care, since he entered upon his duties, to give paramount attention to the numerous and important questions which, in their relations to the state of insurrection that exists in a portion of the territory of Cuba, may lead to excesses of authority, arbitrary acts more or less grave, or the employment of force against the personality of the inhabitants, all of which are, unfortunately, too frequent in the history of all internecine struggles.

Upon undertaking to study these questions, in the fulfillment of one of the first duties of his office, the minister of the colonies found, and could do no less than seek to reform, a state of things, in his judgment, completely anomalous, namely, the existence of a great accumulation of property, wrested from the hands of the legitimate owners with no other formality than a simple executive order, and turned over to an administrative control exercised with great irregularity in the name of the government, to the notable depreciation of the products of those estates, to the injury of the families dependent thereon for support, and to the detriment of the public wealth, whose diminution is the inevitable result of a want of regularity and order, and the absence or withdrawal of individual interests in the control and management of property.

Such a condition of things, besides being utterly at variance with a political system whose fundamental basis must ever be justice, stern, yet considerate, removed from the rancor of party spirit, and foreign to all motives of passion, could lead to no other result than to embitter mutual resentments more and more by the sad spectacle of misery, the more keenly felt as it has been the more suddenly and unexpectedly brought about, and must, moreover, tend to render profitless a great part of the rich soil of the island, and to introduce disturbance and disorder into the system of production, thus interfering with its due development.

The Cuban insurgents, those in correspondence and relations with them, and those who, more or less openly, lend them protection and aid, thus contributing to prolong a cruel, bloody, and destructive war, doubtless merit energetic suppression and exemplary punishment, and the more so to-day, when the government of the republic pledges to all citizens of Spain, on either side of the seas, assured and efficacious guarantees of respect for the rights of all, and offers the means of maintaining their opinions, and propagating them, and causing their ideas to triumph in the only manner in which ideas can triumph in a social structure, raised upon the solid foundations of reason, truth, and right.

But even the need of such punishment can confer upon no government the power to deprive those of its citizens who stray from the right path of their individual means of support, and to enforce upon their families the bitter necessity of begging to-day the bread that abounded but yesterday on their tables as the fruit of their labor or their economy.

Apart from the foregoing considerations, there cannot be found in international law (derecho de gentes) any precept or principle authorizing this class of seizures which bear upon their face the stamp of confiscation; neither under any sound judicial theory is it admissible to proceed in such a manner; nor yet can the exceptional state of war authorize, under any pretext, the adoption of preventive measures of such transcendent importance, and whose results, on the other hand, will inevitably be diametrically opposed to the purpose that inspired them.

In consideration, therefore, of the facts thus set forth, the undersigned minister presents for the approval of the counsel the following draft of a decree.

Madrid, July 12, 1873.

The Minister of the Colonies,

FRANCISCO SUNER Y CAPDEVILA.

### DECREE.

In consideration of the representations set forth by the minister of the colonies, the government of the republic decrees the following:

ARTICLE I. All embargoes put upon the property of insurgents and disloyal persons (*infidentes*) in Cuba, by executive order in consequence of the decree of April 20, 1869, are declared removed from the date when this present decree, published in the Madrid Gazette, shall reach the capital of the island of Cuba.

ARTICLE II. All property disembargoed, by virtue of the provisions of the preceding article, shall be forthwith delivered up to its owners or legal representatives, without requiring from them any other justification or formality than such as may be necessary to show the right under which they claim its restoration, or for their personal identification.

ARTICLE III. In order that questions growing out of the preceding provisions may be decided with greater accuracy and dispatch, the captain general, superior civil governor of the island of Cuba, shall forthwith proceed to organize, under his own chairmanship, a board composed of the president of the audiencia as vice-chairman, the intendente of Cuba, the civil governor of Havana, the attorney-general (fiscal) of the audiencia, and the secretary of the superior civil government, who shall act as secretary of the board, having voice and vote therein; and this board shall summarily, and in the shortest possible time, decide upon such applications as may be made by the interested parties, without any other appeal than the one that may be taken to the government of the republic through the colonial ministry.

ARTICLE IV. The board of authorities charged, under the foregoing article, with the disembargo and restoration of property of insurgents and disloyal persons may, whenever it shall appear needful to the more thorough decision of these questions, consult the board of the public debt (*junta de la deuda del tesoro*), heretofore charged with the administration of property embargoed by executive order, and may ask and obtain from the tribunals of every jurisdiction, and from all other dependencies of the State, the data and antecedents which may be deemed needful to such decision.

ARTICLE V. The minister of the colonies shall issue the necessary instructions for the execution of the present decree, or shall definitively approve those which may be prepared to the same end by the board of disembargoes.

Madrid, July 12, 1873.

The President of the Government of the Republic,

FRANCISCO PI Y MARGALL.

The Minister of the Colonies,

FRANCISCO SUNER Y CAPDEVILA.

4

(Parte oficial.)

GOBIERNO SUPERIOR DE LA PROVINCIA DE CUBA.—SECRETARÍA.

El Excmo. Sr. Ministro de Ultramar, en comunicacion fecha de ayer, dice al Excmo. Sr. Gobernador Superior Político lo que sigue:

" EXCMO. SR : El Gobierno de la República, decidido á procurar la fiel observancia de los tratados y convenios celebrados por España con las naciones extranjeras, deseoso de evitar todo motivo de reclamacion de los naturales de ellas, y movido de las razones que tuvo presente el Consejo de Ministros al dirigir al antecesor de V. E. en el mando de esta Isla, el telégrama de 15 de setiembre último, ha tenido á bien resolver que ordene V. E. el inmediato y extricto cumplimiento de la medida dictada por el Ministerio de mi cargo, disponiendo el desembargo de los bienes de ciudadanos extranjeros, realizado en consecuencia de resolucion gubernativa : á fin de que desde luego puedan entrar los interesados en posesion de dichos bienes. De órden del expresado Gobierno lo digo á V. E. para los efectos correspondientes."

Lo que de órden de S. E. se inserta en la Gaceta para general conocimiento.

Habana, 24 de noviembre de 1873.

El Secretario,

E. COROMINAS CORNELL.

NOTE No. 14.

*Decree ordering the sale of the property ordered to be released.*

(De Oficio.)

INTENDENCIA GENERAL DE HACIENDA.

EXCMO. SR: Allegar recursos para el Erario, sobre el cual pesan obligaciones ineludibles, sin lastimar profundamente los intereses generales de la provincia, y disminuir de un modo positivo la deuda del Tesoro, causa principal de todos los temores y de todas las incertidumbres que inspira el estado económico de este pais, ha sido el objeto de los estudios ó investigaciones de la Intendencia de Hacienda, desde que tiene la señalada honra de dirigir el que suscribe sus complicadas operaciones, si no con gran suma de acierto, con una voluntad excelente al ménos.

La Intendencia cree que es de absoluta necesidad, para que vengan á la circulacion valores metálicos, que desaparezcan los fiduciarios que el Tesoro ha garantido.

La forma en que esto ha de verificarse, para no producir una perturbacion en los mercados, no es asunto del adjunto proyecto de decreto, porque la Intendencia no se propone que desaparezcan en absoluto los billetes de banco emitidos por su cuenta, sin abrigar la seguridad de obtener por otros procedimientos los valores metálicos que aquel papel representa, y estos procedimientos exigen por su importancia la sancion del Gobierno Supremo de la República.

Pero puede darse un paso muy conveniente en la solucion de este problema, procediéndose inmediatamente á la venta de todos los bienes y valores de que se ha incautado la Hacienda por consecuencia de la insurreccion, que constituyen una propiedad del Estado, y consagrándose sus productos á amortizar una buena parte de la deuda representada en los billetes que ha emitido el Banco Español por cuenta de la Hacienda.

La insurreccion separatista es la que ha ocasionado la crísis del Tesoro, la creacion de los valores fiduciarios y la situacion anormal de las operaciones comerciales y de toda transaccion mercantil; y siendo esto innegable, nada más natural que consagrar el valor de esas propiedades á amortizar una parte de la deuda, resultando de aquí no sólo un beneficio para el Estado que se libra de los detalles minuciosos que ocasiona la administracion de esas propiedades y una economía por consiguiente, en el presupuesto de gastos, sino tambien una gran ventaja para el interés privado que encuentra una nueva y legítima especulacion, para promover los adelantos en la riqueza del pais.

Por exquisita que sea la fiscalizacion del Estado en la administracion de estas propiedades, no es posible que den los resultados que pueden obtenerse, los productos que pueden alcanzarse, como no se lleven esos valores y esas propiedades al desenvolvimiento que produce el interés individual, y esta doctrina ajustada al principio económico de que debe desamortizarse todo lo amortizado, es tanto mas applicable al presente caso, cuanto que el Estado no debe administrar prédio rústico, ni fincas urbanas, ni constituirse en custodio de otros valores que aquellos que producen los impuestos ó de los que se crean como operaciones del Tesoro.

Con la inmediata realizacion de este pensamiento, la Administracion Económica de esta Isla queda exenta de una porcion de trabajos que la impiden reflejar toda su accion en asunto de vital interés y se obtiene el no pequeño beneficio de disminuir en una cantidad respetable la deuda del Tesoro.

Habana, 2 de setiembre de 1873.

El Intendente general,

M. CRESPO QUINTANA.

DECRETO.

En atencion á las consideraciones expuestas por la Intendencia general de Hacienda, en su consulta de 2 del actual, vengo en disponer lo siguiente:

ARTICULO 1º. Se procederá inmediatamente á la venta en subasta pública de todos los bienes, propiedades y valores de que se ha incautado la Hacienda por consecuencia de la insurreccion.

ARTICULO 2º. Los productos integros de la venta de estos bienes, valores y propiedades, se dedicarán exclusivamente á amortizar una parte de la deuda del Tesoro, sacando de la circulacion billetes emitidos por cuenta del Estado.

ARTICULO 3º. Respecto de los bienes que se hallan en arrendamiento, la venta de estos se verificará sin daño de anteriores contratos.

ARTICULO 4º. La Intendencia de Hacienda dictará las órdenes necesarias para la inmediata ejecucion de este decreto.

Habana, 3 de setiembre de 1873.

CANDIDO PIELTAIN.

NOTE No. 15.

*Another decree to the same effect.*

INTENDENCIA GENERAL DE HACIENDA.

Son tan graves y perentorias las atenciones del Estado, hay tantos problemas pendientes de solucion satisfactoria, es tan sagrado el deber que para con la Historia, para con la Pátria y para con la Sociedad hay contraido á nombre de España en esta apartada provincia, que es urgente llegar sin pérdida de tiempo al terreno práctico de lo dispuesto en el decreto de 3 del actual sobre la venta de bienes incautados.

Indisputable es la plenitud de derecho, la acrisola da justicia que ha precedido á su promulgacion, y no debe defraudarse en manera alguna la espectacion pública, deteniendo en largas tramitaciones la realizacion de lo mandado, sino que, por el contrario, la Intendencia cree estar en el deber de asumir desde luego todas sus facultades, y considerando como son en realidad bienes del Estado los que fueron de los enemigos de España, proceder á su enajenacion por la via ordinaria, por que as lo demanda la justicia, porque así lo exige el Estado del Tesoro, las contrataciones mercantiles y la fortuna pública.

Grande, inmensa seria la responsabilidad de los que habiendo lanzado á la publicidad aquel importante decreto, se detuviesen hoy para realizarlo en dificultades de trámite que jamás deben detener la accion de la justicia, ni el honrado propósito de procurar el bien público, De un modo análogo se procedió en 1841 por las Autoridades de esta isla á la supresion de las órdenes religiosas y venta de sus bienes.

En su virtud y teniende en cuenta lo dispuesto en la ley de contratacion de servicios públicos da 1852, en el decreto de 25 de julio de 1862, para la enagenacion de bienes del Estado y Reglamento para la venta de 29 de setiembre de 1864, usando de la autorizacion que me ha sido otorgada en el decreto de 3 del actual por el Excmo. Sr. Gobernador Superior Civil, he acordado lo siguiente :

1º. Se crea una Junta especial de venta de bienes incautados que se compondrá del

Intendente—Presidente.

Administrador Central de Rentas.

Contador Central de Hacienda.

Alcalde mayor decano.

Promotor fiscal idem.

Ponente del Consejo de Administracion, que además de Vocal ejercerá las funciones de Consultor.

2º. La Junta entenderá desde luego en todo lo relativo á la enajenacion de los bienes y valores incautados que custodia y administra la Junta de la Deuda.

3º. Para la parte administrativa se crea además una seccion especial encargada de tramitar con arreglo á instruccion todos los expedientes de venta, la cual funcionará bajo la dependencia directiva de esta Intendencia, siendo secretario de la Junta el jefe de esta Comision.

4º. La Comision, que será parte integrante de la Intendencia, llevará una contabilidad ajustada en todo al Decreto del Regente del Reino de 12 de setiembre de 1870.

5º. Se procederá desde luego á la venta en pública licitacion de todos los valores que no hayan menester prévia tasacion de peritos.

6º. Los valores de que se trata empezarán á venderse dentro de quince dias, para lo cual funcionará desde luego la Junta y Comision que se crean por el presente decreto.

7º. La Comision de venta formará sin pérdida de tiempo los oportunos expedientes para emprender con la misma actividad la tasacion, licitacion y remate de los valores que haya menester de estos trámites.

8º. Las licitaciones y remates en general tendrán lugar á los quence dias de publicados los anuncios de ventas en la Gaceta oficial de esta capital, y en los demás puntos donde deban oirse proposiciones á los ocho dias de la llegada del correo, cuya operacion será simultánea.

9º. La licitacion general es en la Habana, y la parcial de los intereses puestos en venta tendrá lugar en la jurisdiccion donde radiquen ante el Alcalde mayor y jefe mas caracterizado de Hacienda.

10º. La Junta publicara quincenalmente en la Gaceta el estado de sus operaciones y disminucion de la Deuda, así como tambien relacion general de los bienes que hayan de venderse.

11º. Los pagos de los valores fiduciarios, muebles y ganados se hará al contado por el total de su importe. Los de fincas rústicas y urbanas y demás bienes en la forma ordinaria.

12º. Todas las tramitaciones á que den lugar las operaciones de venta se ajustarán, en aquello que no se oponga al presente decreto, al de 25 de julio de 1862, por el que fueron declarados en estado de venta todos los prédios rústicos y urbanos, solares y censos que pertenecieron á las órdenes religiosas, Reglamento de 29 de setiembre de 1864 y demás disposiciones vigentes.

13º. Las oficinas de Hacienda en aquello que las concierna, dictarán las órdenes oportunas al cumplimiento de lo mandado.

Habana, 11 de Setiembre de 1863.

El Intendente general.

M. CRESPO QUINTANA.

## NOTE No. 16.

*Decree for the unconditional release of all property seized.*

SECRETARIA—POLITICA.

El Excmo. Sr. Ministro de Ultramar con fecha 16 de Julio último comunica al Excmo. Sr. Gobernador General la Real órden siguiente:

" EXCMO. SR.: En vista del telegrama de V. E. de 20 de Junio último, solicitando que, como consecuencia de las disposiciones del bando que dictó en 24 de marzo anterior, siendo General en Jefe del Ejército de operaciones de esa Isla, se le autorice para devolver todos los bienes incautados por delitos de infidencia sin las limitaciones impuestas por el artículo 4º. del Real Decreto de 20 de octubre del año próximo pasado, S. M. el Rey (q. D. g.) ha tenido á bien disponer, de acuerdo con el Consejo de Ministros, la derogacion de lo preceptuado en dicho artículo 4º. del referido Real Decreto de 20 de octubre de 1877.—De Real órden lo digo á V. E. para su cumplimiento y efectos que correspondan."

Y acordado su cumplimiento por S. E. con fecha de ayer, se inserta en la Gaceta oficial para general conocimiento.

Habana 9 de agosto de 1878.

R. GALBIS.

48

NOTE No. 17.

No. 2.

*Mr. Plumb to Mr. Davis.*

CONSULATE-GENERAL OF THE UNITED STATES,
HAVANA, *August* 17, 1869.

The telegram, of which a copy is annexed hereto, reached me in the evening of the 13th instant.

In compliance with the instruction therein contained, I called upon the Captain-General on Monday the 15th instant, and in consideration of the reference made to the Spanish minister I gave him the telegram to read.

He replied to me that the embargo of property is not confiscation, but detention, in such manner that no revenue from or avails of the property can reach the custody or disposition of the parties against whom the proceeding is taken.

That in the case of real estate the embargo does not prevent its legal descent by inheritance, and although not so provided in the dispositions upon the subject placed in force here, in certain cases an allowance is now being made from the revenue of embargoed property for the support of the family of the person embargoed.

That if the proceedings taken can be shown to be without just foundation, the property will be released, and the government will hold itself responsible for the revenues or proceeds it may have received.

\*    \*    \*    \*    \*    \*    \*

No. 3.

*No.* 126.   *Mr. Plumb to Mr. Davis.*

HAVANA, *August* 25, 1869.

I have also been informed by the political secretary that in the case of persons residing out of the island whose property has been embargoed upon evidence received by the government that they are taking part in the insurrection, their means of rebutting this evidence should be the presentation before the Spanish consul of the place where they reside of evidence by testimony of trustworthy persons that they are not so compromised, and that such evidence transmitted to the captain-general will weigh towards the removal of the embargo, if the ground upon which it has been based proves to be not well founded.

By the present mail I hope to be able to send to the department the full collection I am preparing of the decrees and orders issued under the present system of embargo of property as a political measure.

Awaiting your instructions, I am, &c., &c.

NOTE No. 18.

*Classification of the cases before the arbitrators.*

In the "statement of the condition of the cases before the United States and Spanish commission," sent to the Senate of the United

States, in compliance with a resolution passed by that august body on the 19th of January, 1880 (Ex. Doc. No. 86, Senate, Forty-sixth Congress, second session), it appears that 131 cases had been referred up to that date to the arbitrators appointed under the agreement of February 12, 1871, between the United States and Spain.

The study of this " statement," completed by the perusal of the records of each case, shows the following:

1st. That out of these 131 cases there are 64 presented by persons who were not born in the island of Cuba. This takes out a great deal of the poison which the advocate of Spain has attempted to infiltrate into the mind of the umpire, by speaking always of "*naturalized Cubans*," and trying to represent them as rebels to Spain, and people animated alone by "deadly hatred" against Spaniards, and by " a semi-insane spirit of chronic rebellion."

Henry Story, Juan F. Machado. born in Brazil; Peter Molière, James M. Edwards, Leopold A. Price, William Montgomery, Lucien Lairgne, Gideon Lowe, George Aab, Felix Bister, Thomas Bister, George Bode, Inocencio Casanova, born in the Canary Islands; Hewlett C. Codwise, Daniel Deshon, Danford Knowlton, Peter V. King, Thomas K. Foster, Dugan, as executor of Compton (No. 39); John Mathews, John Wyeth, George W. Wingate, Augustus Wilson, James H. West, Andrew D. White, Harry Norris, John Nenninger, born in Baltimore; and the consul of Sweden and Norway, in Havana; Augustus E. Phillips, Margaret C. Speakman, Silas M. Stillwell, John Shannon, Henry G. Smith, Dr. A. T. Simmons, E. G. Schmidt, Moses Taylor & Co., Henry T. Street, Peter Glaube, Joseph Griffin, Waydell & Co., William A. Jones, Hugh Johnston, Charles A. Campbell, the ship Mary Lowell; Youngs, Smith & Co., Danford, Knowlton & Co. (second case); Danford, Knowlton, and Peter V. King & Co. (second case); John Francis Cahill, John Dolis, Vincent Nenninger, Felix Bister, William S. Lynn, William D. Foulke, John E. Powers, John Emile Howard, Charles Jemot, William W. Cox *et al.* (No. 109); William W. Cox (No. 110); Galatea Marot, V. Eugene Bennet, Alfred G. Compton, Joseph O. Wilson, J. F. Machado (No. 129); Danford, Knowlton & Co. (No. 130); Knowlton & Co. and King & Co. (No. 131). Total, 64 cases of reclamations, by persons either native citizens of the United States, or by naturalized citizens of the United States not born in Cuba.

2d. That out of the balance of 67 cases, twenty-four were presented as growing out of personal damages, imprisonment, exile, destruction of property by military operations, &c., as follows:

Brito, Cabias, Cabada, Rozas, Polhemus, Gregorio Gonzalez, José Manuel Ponce de Leon, José Maria Ortega, Patchot, Portuondo, Santa Rosa, Emilio de Silva, Estrada (see list in Foreign Relations of the United States in 1871, page 715), and Casanova Brothers, Fritot, Luna, Lanza, Carret, José M. Casanova, San Pedro, Montejo, Rafael Casanova, Ruiz, Zaldinar. Total, 24 cases, having nothing to do with the embargoes.

3d. That, out of the balance of 43 cases, there are only four arising out of *judicial embargoes* under the decree of September, 1869, followed by confiscation, under the decision of the council of war of November 7, 1870, to wit: Ramon Fernandez Criado y Gomez, No. 29 ; Joaquin M. Delgado, No. 31 ; Antonio Maximo Mora, No. 48, and Francisco C. Yzquierdo, No. 7.

4th. That the balance of 41 cases, arising out of *executive* embargoes, under the decrees of April, 1869, admits of the following classification :

4 SP

A. Cases in which the property has been restored to claimants, and claimants demand nothing:

Bachiller, Bello. F. Guiteras, R. M. Hernandez, Martin Mueses, Thomas J. Mora, Paulina Alfonso de Mestre, Manuel Prieto, Valdes, Placencia, Isaac Carrillo y O'Farrill, Perfecto de Rojas. Total, 12 cases.

B. Cases in which the property has been restored, and awards have been made by the arbitrators or the umpires:

Joaquin Garcia de Angarica, Fernando Dominguez, José de Jesus Fernandez y Macias, Gonzalo Poey ; total, 4 cases.

C. Cases in which the property—that is to say, the estates—have been restored, but the income has been retained and no damages paid, to wit:

Felix Govin, No. 9 ; Manuel Rojas, Rivas y Lamar, José Govin, Madan ; total, 5 cases.

D. Miscellaneous cases : J. G. Delgado, No. 12 and No. 125, Manuel G. Angarica, Enrique Valiente, Alfaya, Bazan, José Garcia Angarica, Buzzi, Mrs. de Mora, Acosta y Foster, Fausto Mora et al., Macias, Dolores Agramente, M. C. Rodrigues & Co., Batlle ; total, 15 cases.

E. Cases either withdrawn or abandoned by claimants, to wit: Pineda, Madeira ; total, 2 cases.

---

### Note No. 19.

*Circular of Chief Justice Calveton.*

#### REGENCIA.

En el discurso de apertura decia " que el valor civico debe ser el distintivo mas precioso del carácter del juez, mayormente en épocas de agitacion." Al enunciar esta verdad tenia por desgracia presentes las circunstancias del momento en esta Isla y las que podian surgir por la série de los acontecimintos. La conducta que debe seguir el Juez es dificil algunas veces : pero esta trazada claramente en la Ley. Cerrar los oidos á sujestiones de todo género, escuchar solo los dictámenes de la razon y los impasibles preceptos de la Ley en medio del tumulto de las pasiones, sea cualquiera su origen, es su deber como Juez. No creo que nadie se atreva á ajecer la menor presion en el animo del Juez cuando está cumpliendo las sagradas funciones de su ministerio ; pero si por desgracia, alguna vez sucediese, espero que V. S. cumplirá dignamente con los severos deberes que su cargó le impone, pidiendo proteccion á la Autoridad gubernativa si la estimarse absolutamente necesaria, y poniendo en conocemiento de las Salas de Justicia y en el mio cualquiera cosa que ocurra en tan trascendental materia teniendo siempre presente que la imparcealidad mas extricta y la prudencia mas exquisita, son las dotes que mas han de resplandecer en todas las providencias que dicte el Juez.

Habana 27 de Enero de 1869.

JOAQUIN CALVETON.

Sres. Alcaldes mayores del territorio.

---

### Note No. 20.

United States of America,
*Department of State :*

To all to whom these presents shall come, greeting :

I certify that the document hereto annexed is a true copy from the files of this Department.

In testimony whereof I, William M. Evarts, Secretary of State of the United States, have hereunto subscribed my name, and caused the seal of the Department of State to be affixed.

Done at the city of Washington this 4th day of March, A. D. 1878, and of the Independence of the United States of America the one hundred and second.

[SEAL.]                              WM. M. EVARTS.

### Mr. Cushing to the Conde de Casa-Valencia.

[Extract.]

LEGATION OF THE UNITED STATES,
*Madrid, October 21, 1875.*

\*     \*     \*     \*     \*     \*     \*

My government conceives that the summary trial of any of its citizens by an ordinary and petty council of war, without the presence of the accused, without such counsel as he may choose, without examination and cross-examination of witnesses by him, is contrary to the express letter of treaty; and it cannot cease to remonstrate and reclaim against all such acts, by whatsoever arguments of erroneously supposed temporary expediency they may be defended. It believes them to be not beneficial, but on the contrary prejudicial to Spain herself, and that these passionate acts of violence of subordinate authorities are no more profitable to Spain in Cuba than to Don Carlos in Spain. It knows that they have always been condemned by the supreme authorities at Madrid. But question of the expediency or inexpediency of such acts from a domestic point of view is quite aside of the merits of the controversy. My government stands on the lofty pedestal of the faith of treaties, and on that it relies; but it also relies on the chivalric sentiments which characterize the true Spaniard, and respectfully but earnestly invokes His Majesty's government not to be untrue to those among the noblest of traditions of the national policy of Spain which gave to the world the great example of protecting within her broad dominions the rights of the subjects of foreign powers.

2. But my government has a heavier charge to bring against the local authorities of Cuba, if it be possible to present a heavier one than violation of the faith of treaties, coupled with dishonor of the most glorious traditions of the public policy of Spain.

Your excellency is a ripe scholar, an experienced diplomatist, a distinguished legislator, a practical statesman, to whom all the principles and maxims of public law are "familiar" as "household words." What would your excellency say if informed that half a dozen respectable Spanish gentlemen, living quietly at their homes on the banks of the Tagus or the Guadalquivir, chiefly occupied, as good and wise men should be, with the care of their wives and children, had been tried for their lives in the United States, in the lump, without notice, and of course without a hearing, by some low tribunal in one of the outlying Territories of the United States, and condemned, in the lump, to death by *garrote vil*, on false and trumped-up accusation of having, in *Spain*, entertained opinions or spoken words adverse to the interests or unacceptable to the pride of the Government of the United States?

Would not your excellency say, "Impossible; it is not credible that a thing so monstrous, so foolish, so contrary to the most elemental principles of the public law and of the international right of Christian Europe and America should have been done by any pretended tribunal in even the obscurest corner of the backwoods of the United States"? And if satisfied that it had been done, would not the Government of His Majesty vehemently insist, without delay of a day, on receiving reparation in the premises from the Government of the United States?

And yet this monstrous, this foolish, this incredible violation of the laws of nations has been perpetrated by the local authorities of Cuba, not in the hot blood of contest in the *manigua*, but coolly, deliberately, in the cultivated capital of the island, and under the very eye of the captain-general.

In view of the provisions of the Constitution of the United States, hereinbefore cited, your excellency will perceive that no such thing could possibly have happened within the jurisdiction of my government.

We cannot try a man without public indictment, unless he belong to the land or sea forces, or the militia in the field. He must be tried by jury; he can only be tried in the State where the offense charged purports to have been committed; and of course he cannot be tried for an act done, or imputed to be done, in a foreign country. He must be confronted with the witnesses; he is to have all customary means of defense by counsel; he is not subject to a council of war, ordinary or extraordinary; and he is under the safeguard of the general laws of the United States.

How much in striking contrast with all these privileges which a Spaniard enjoys in the United States is the unimaginable procedure in question applied to citizens of the United States in Cuba!

Here is no question of the applicability of Spanish laws to foreigners residing or sojourning in the dominions of Spain, and so subject to its jurisdiction. It is quite a different matter.

Nearly five years have elapsed since the first instance of this most wrongful procedure was practiced in Cuba (and other cases have since occurred) with reference to citizens of the United States, they being within the United States—men utterly void of offense—and on false accusations of words uttered within the United States. My government protested immediately on receiving information of such unprecedented wrong. And the written remonstrance on the subject addressed by my predecessor to the minister of state of the Spanish Government has not yet, so far as I can discover, received any fit response, nor scarcely even the grace of deliberate notice.

It is sometimes imputed that my government is importunate in such matters. I do not think so. A wrong of signal enormity is perpetrated on our citizens; we make respectful representations on the subject, and at the end of five years we not only have obtained no redress, but we have not obtained even a due hearing of our representations. And we still wait for it. Is not that a rare example of patience?

Five years! Twenty five ministries! Yes. I admit that during the most part of those five years Spain has been racked in the throes of revolution; she has not been really in possession of herself; ephemeral governments have passed across the stage of her national life, one after another, which "come like shadows, so depart."

Be it so; and the United States have, with sincere good-will, borne all this in mind and waited accordingly, even while similar violations of justice were being repeated. But we presume that we are not now in the presence of a phantom government. We understand that His Majesty the King comes to sweep away rubbish and ruins—to restore, to renovate, to rebuild—to replace the Spain of so many illustrious ancestral Alfonsos within the great concert of the nations of Europe, where she rightfully belongs, and where the general good of Christendom requires she should be ; and we appeal to him through the organ of your excellency to exert his royal will for the removal of these "stumbling-blocks and rocks of offense," placed by wrongful and unfaithful subordinate officers of past governments in the path of the amicable intercourse of Spain and the United States.

I respectfully solicit the candid consideration of these observations, and avail myself of the occasion to reiterate to your excellency the assurance of my most distinguished consideration.

C. CUSHING.

His Excellency the MINISTER OF STATE.

---

*Mr. Fernando Calderon y Collantes, Minister of State ad interim, to Mr. Cushing.*

[Translation.]

MINISTRY OF STATE,
*The Palace, November 15, 1875.*
(Received November 16, 1875, 3 p. m.)

EXCELLENCY:

SIR:   *   *   *   *   *   *   *

The government of the King does not regard as justiciable, before the Spanish tribunals, the citizens of the United States, or of any other state, for the crimes or faults which they commit, or which they may commit, within their own national territory. There is no room, therefore, in this respect, for discordance of opinions between the United States and Spain; and the government of the King is prepared to immediately annul all the criminal proceedings, if there be such, which may have been instituted against genuine citizens of the United States, legitimately sheltered by their government against whatsoever error or abuse of foreign tribunals. The undersigned will collect, therefore, all the antecedents which exist in this behalf in the ministry under his charge, and will carefully examine all the particular cases to which the predecessor of your excellency referred, and such as your excellency's self may present to him in the future, with the most firm resolve to immediately make due amends (*desagraviar*) to the United States, provided that, in the matter treated of, they have real and unredressed wrongs.

For the delays hitherto experienced in this matter, and which your excellency himself attributes to the short duration of the Spanish governments in these last years, the actual ministers of the King are assuredly not responsible. Our nation is, without doubt, responsible for it, as, in fact, are all her discords and civil wars; but as there is probably no nation which has not passed through like crises and misfortunes in the course, equity, which is, for certain, the juridical foundation of the law of nations, has already designated, and by common consent, the limits within which, in such cases, a government may be responsible for the omissions, perhaps involuntary, of its predecessors.

*   *   *   *   *   *   *

FERN'DO CALDERON Y COLLANTES.

The MINISTER PLENIPOTENTIARY OF THE UNITED STATES.

No. 118.]                         LEGATION OF THE UNITED STATES,
                                        *Madrid, February* 10, 1876.

SIR: I transmit herewith the correspondence between myself and the minister of state on the subject of the "confiscation cases," of the prompt settlement of which by the Spanish Government you have already been informed by telegraph.

You will understand that the "Memorandum" annexed was but the text of oral representations made by me to the minister of state, which, however, it seems to me unnecessary to repeat in view of the full and satisfactory settlement of the whole question.

I have the honor to be, very respectfully, your obedient servant,
                                        O. CUSHING.
The honorable HAMILTON FISH,
                *Secretary of State.*

---

APPENDIX A, No. 118.

*Memorandum of confiscation cases, handed to the Minister of State January* 31, 1876.

(Copy.)

Memorandum of certain cases of citizens of the United States condemned to death in Cuba while in the United States, or now under charge for acts or words of *infidencia* charged (falsely) to have been committed or uttered in the United States, with confiscation of property.

Joaquin Delgado.
Ramon Fernandez Criado y Gomez.
Antonio Mora.
Magdalena Farrés de Mora.

1. The three persons first named are included in a sentence of November 8, 1870, condemning to death fifty-four persons *en masse*. The fourth is the wife of one of the three under process but not yet sentenced, and her property is under seizure.

2. The three citizens of the United States named were condemned on the *report* only of being members of the Cuban Junta, or, as the principal witness says, "spoken of as members of the junta, or at least auxiliaries and friends of the same."

3. A similar charge is made against Mrs. Mora, but is also false.

3. These four cases are of the class of condemnations which his excellency Mr. Calderon y Collantes, in his note of November 15th last, admits to be in flagrant violation of justice and of the rights of the United States.

5th. The undersigned respectfully suggests that the prompt solution of these four cases of crying injustice, of four years' standing, will constitute a decisive step in the direction of peaceful relations between the United States and Spain.

Legation of the United States of America, Madrid, January 31, 1876.
    (Signed)                                    C. CUSHING.

APPENDIX C, No. 819.

*Mr. Calderon y Collantes to Mr. Cushing.*

[Translation.]

MINISTRY OF STATE,
Palace, January 31, 1876.  (Rec'd February 1, 1876.)

EXCELLENCY:

SIR: I have received the memorandum which, under date of to-day, your excellency has been pleased to address to me relative to several sentences in cases of *infidencia* pronounced against citizens of the United States and embargo of their properties in Cuba.

So soon as I shall have acquainted myself with the antecedents of this affair, I shall have the honor to bring to your excellency's knowledge the resolution of the government, improving meanwhile this occasion to reiterate to your excellency the assurances of my most distinguished consideration.

(Signed)  FERN'DO CALDERON Y COLLANTES.

Señor MINISTER PLENIPOTENTIARY OF THE UNITED STATES.

---

APPENDIX D, No. 818.

(Copy.)

*Mr. Cushing to Mr. Calderon y Collantes.*

LEGATION OF THE UNITED STATES,
Madrid, February 6, 1876.

SIR: In reference to the cases specified in my memorandum of the 31st ultimo, permit me to explain, as follows:

I am instructed by my government to declare that it appears by evidence filed in the Department of State of the United States that Joaquin Delgado was naturalized in due form of law as a citizen of the United States on the 5th of November, 1866; that Ramon Fernandez Criado y Gomez was in like manner duly naturalized on the 15th of April, 1869; and that Antonio Maximo Mora was in like manner duly naturalized on the 14th of May, 1869.

It further appears, by proof on file in the said department, that Magdalena Farrés de Mora, wife of the aforesaid Antonio Mora, and a citizen of the United States, was, at or about the same period, made the subject of military process in Cuba for (falsely charged) acts of *infidencia* against Spain, on which property, belonging to her in her own right, was seized and is still withheld, she being at the time a citizen of the United States, and actually in the United States; but that no final sentence was ever entered in the proceedings, which served only as a pretext for the detention of the property of the said Magdalena Farrés de Mora.

The attention of the Spanish Government was called to these cases soon after they occurred; that is, in the epoch of the regency, but nothing was then done in the premises.

Subsequently it was supposed that these cases had been disposed of by the Spanish decree of disembargo of 1873 and subsequent diplomatic arrangements between the two governments; but the supposition turned out to be erroneous on its appearing. that the cases were not of mere embargo by gubernative authority, but of process of confiscation.

I need not repeat here the arguments applicable to these cases, addressed to your excellency in my note of the 20th of October last, conceiving that all discussion on the subject is rendered superfluous by the frank and honorable admission of the illegal character of the proceedings therein made by your excellency in the note of the 16th of November.

I will only add that the cases of this class, two of them by express name, are specially mentioned as examples of signal wrong, in the dispatch addressed to me by Mr. Fish, of the 5th of November, and communicated to your excellency; and I need not enlarge, therefore, on the obvious considerations which invoke for them the early attention of your excellency.

I avail myself of this occasion to reiterate to your excellency the assurance of my most distinguished consideration.

(Signed)                                                  C. CUSHING.
His Excellency the MINISTER OF STATE.

---

APPENDIX F, No. 818.

*Mr. Calderon y Collantes to Mr. Cushing.*

[Translation.]

MINISTRY OF STATE,
*Palace, February 9, 1876.*   (Rec'd February 9, 1876, 2 p. m.)

EXCELLENCY:

SIR: On the 31st of January last, I had the honor to acknowledge reception of the memorandum which, under the same date, your excellency was pleased to address to me in response to the process and condemnation of the American subjects, Joaquin Delgado, Ramon Fernandez, Criado y Gomez, Antonio Mora, and Magdalena Farrés de Mora.

I have now the satisfaction to inform your excellency that the government of His Majesty, accepting as sufficient proof of the nationality of those persons the data set forth by your excellency's communication dated the 6th instant, seeing that the Spanish laws do not concede to the executive power the right of annulling sentences made executory, has resolved to remit and pardon the penalty which was imposed on the above-named subjects of the United States by the ordinary council of war, and in consequence thereof to command that there be immediately raised the confiscation or embargo of their property which may have been decreed, leaving it at their free disposal.

The resolution of the government of His Majesty is communicated this very day by telegraph to the superior authorities of Cuba, and your excellency may rest assured that it will be faithfully executed.

The government of His Majesty hopes that in this resolution that of the United States will see a proof of the sincerity with which Spain desires to attend, with justice and promptness, to all the reclamations addressed to it, and of its earnest care in maintaining friendly rela-

57

tions with all foreign governments, removing for its part whatever obstacles may oppose themselves to this satisfactory result, so convenient for all.

I improve this opportunity to reiterate to your excellency the assurances of my most distinguished consideration.

(Signed) FERNDO. CALDERON Y COLLANTES.

Señor MINISTER OF THE UNITED STATES.

APPENDIX G, No. 818.

(Copy.)

*Mr. Cushing to Mr. Calderon y Collantes.*

LEGATION OF THE UNITED STATES,
*Madrid, February 9, 1876.*

SIR: It has afforded me lively satisfaction to receive your excellency's note of this date, communicating to me the prompt resolution of His Majesty's government in the matter of the confiscated property of certain citizens of the United States, which had been so long unattended to by previous governments.

I have already transmitted information thereof to my government by telegraph, and shall dispatch the correspondence on the subject by mail, not doubting that the President of the United States will duly appreciate the friendly purposes and good faith manifested in this respect by His Majesty's government.

I avail myself of this occasion to reiterate to your excellency the expression of my most distinguished consideration.

(Signed) C. CUSHING.

His Excellency the MINISTER OF STATE.

5 SP

ngramcontent.com/pod-product-compliance
ng Source LLC
ersburg PA
021638270326
CB00008B/1073